Good Broth to Warm Our Bones

Good Broth to Warm Our Bones

Hugh Steven

CROSSWAY BOOKS • WESTCHESTER, ILLINOIS
A DIVISION OF GOOD NEWS PUBLISHERS

PUBLISHED IN COOPERATION WITH
WYCLIFFE ASSOCIATES

Cover design and illustration by Britt Taylor Collins.

First printing, 1982
Second printing, 1983

Printed in the United States of America.

Library of Congress Catalog Card Number 82-71182
ISBN 0-89107-297-7

Acknowledgments

When a writing project is over, particularly a long project, it is often difficult to recall all those who contributed insights and helpful anecdotes. Therefore, with apologies to those who contributed but are not here named, I thank them.

There were a few people, however, like Don and Thelma Webster, Turner Blount, Alan Pence and Roy Ahmaogak who provided material indispensable to the writing of this book, and I thank them.

I would like also to thank Dr. Wayne Halleen for his fine tuning of my medical knowledge. Also to the men of my Wednesday morning prayer group who prayed for and encouraged me in my journeys and in the long periods of solitude that are required to produce a book.

I thank as well Jan Dennis, Editor-in-Chief of Crossway Books, for his creativity and encouragement—to him belongs the credit for the book's title—and because he is a true friend of literature.

Finally to Norma my wife, my most helpful critic and without whose love, encouragement, and practical help I would surely perish.

Contents

To the memory of
Roy Ahmaogak
whom God set apart from birth and by His grace called
to reveal his Son among His people (Galatians 1:15-16)

and

Mary Ellen "Nanauk" Webster
who came briefly as a bright gift of light and who gave to her
parents happiness in her life, consecration in her trial, and in
her death, direction to glory (2 Corinthians 4:17).

Preface

They were young, as I was young, when I first met Don and Thelma Webster at the Summer Institute of Linguistics in the summer of 1956. For Don and Thelma it was to be a summer of study and romance that led first to a commitment to serve with Wycliffe, and then to each other in marriage.

Later, as newlyweds, they, along with a core of soon-to-be Wycliffe workers that included my wife and myself, experienced Wycliffe's Jungle Training Camp, then held in southern Mexico. By this time the Websters had become special friends, the kind of "special" that binds people together when they experience shared hardship.

After Jungle Camp, we each went to our fields of assignment—Websters to Alaska; my wife and I to Mexico. As the years passed, we heard snitches and snatches of what God was doing and had done in and through them. I didn't see Don again until 1966. He and Roy Ahmaogak had come to Mexico for a special Bible translation workshop. I was just beginning a new career as an author and asked Don if I could write his story. Characteristically open and guileless, Don said thanks but no thanks. He thought he might write his own story. I accepted that as God's will and proceeded to write the book, "Manuel." Thirteen years later in 1979, Don and I found ourselves serving together on the same Board of Directors of Wycliffe's Canada Division. During a lull in the meeting one day, I again asked Don if he was open to having his story written. This time he said yes.

After researching and delving into the Websters' lives, I began to realize how right it was for me to have waited these thirteen years. God knew I needed more experience, particularly in knowing how to empathize with those in sorrow (I gained deep insight from my own daughter's near death experience during the beginning of this writing project). As always God's timing was perfect. And as always, as one who is privileged to walk into the lives of people at such a deep and emotive level, I became richer.

The following is an excerpt from the chapter, "Living Without Answers." As Don worked through a difficult period in his life, his thoughts about God and reality and faith tumbled out in a kind of soliloquy . . .

Living faith must be positive and expectant if it is to be effective. But at the same time we must allow for God's sovereignty. One of the best ways to come to terms with life's paradoxes is to celebrate our dependence upon God by accepting the paradoxes. Christians are called to live their lives by faith, which means we live our lives without demanding answers to our questions. It should be enough that God knows the end from the beginning and ultimately has our best interests at heart.

Here then is a book about three people—Don, Thelma, and Roy Ahmaogak, who in their encounter with God, with life, with vocation, and with each other, show us what is often difficult to define: *the nature of true courage*.

Prologue

For centuries the Inupiat Eskimos have lived in tiny village clusters all along Alaska's North Slope—from Kotzebue, to Point Hope, to Wainwright and Barrow, and eastward to Demarcation Point on the Alaskan-Canadian boundary. And for centuries these semi-nomadic hunters and gatherers of the treeless arctic desert have been hunters supreme.

Coupling raw courage with ingenious tools like the harpoon with its detachable head, and skin boats with waterproof hand-sewn blind seams, the Inupiat sets out to harvest the fruits of his inhospitable land. In particular, the Inupiat's chief prize is the bowhead, or "right" whale. This astonishing fifty- to sixty-five-foot animal that weighs in at a ton for every foot, is to the Inupiat what the buffalo was to the Plains Indians—their very survival. Without the bowhead there would be no oil, thus there would be no light or heat in their homes. But more importantly, there would be no food. The thick black skin and delicately pink blubber or *muktuk* of a single whale will keep an Inupiat community alive through the long brutal Arctic winter. But there are other subsistence animals to harvest—the hair or ringed seal, or the formidable bearded or *ugruk* seal that can at 800 pounds drag an unprepared Inupiat off an open lead into a cold watery grave. And the walrus. Those who hunt them must possess extraordinary ability. Weighing up to a ton, the walrus is one of the most fearless and powerful animals in the Arctic.

There are other animals, of course. Animals important for Inupiat clothing, like the caribou, polar bear, fox, wolverine, and wolf. To be Inupiat means to be preoccupied with the daily struggle against starvation. It means to live a semi-nomadic life-style, moving in rhythm with the changing seasons, to go where fish and game are or where the Inupiat hope they will be.

Unfortunately, more times than most Inupiat want to remember, food supply isn't always where they think. For reasons unexplained, the caribou might suddenly change their spring and fall migratory route. Or the bowhead will forget to plough down the lead (the opening of water between two masses of ice) where they are camped. And sometimes when an Inupiat spots a bowhead, he is frustrated when the wind changes and slams the lead shut: he can hear the harsh breathing underfoot as the whale sounds, but can only stand helpless, unable to harvest what he knows is indispensable for his very existence.

To be Inupiat also means to be preoccupied with survival in one of earth's most fearsome climates, where cold becomes intense enough to drive men mad. For the Inupiat live at the very edge of a treacherous frozen world where the slightest change in climate can tip the precarious balance of life.

Their front door opens onto the Arctic Ocean—five million square miles of ice and snow and wind and fog and strong currents that play life and death tricks on all who venture onto its breast. And to be Inupiat means to have no choice but to venture into this world of stark beauty and craggy glittering ice. A world of sudden gales that tear at fragile man. A world of whiteout blizzards, so blinding a hunter is unable to see his own feet. A world where there is constant danger of slipping off the ice into the cold black waters of an open lead and being swept away by a current strong enough to move hundred-ton ice floes as easily as if they were child's building blocks. A world of endless snow and ice where even the most experienced hunters sometimes never return.

Yet juxtaposed between this real and evident danger, is another meaning. To be Inupiat is to be a hunter, and little else gives an Inupiat man a greater sense of fulfillment. It is through the hunt that he achieves a sense of aliveness and psychological completeness. It is through the hunt that he reaches his potential for prestige and maturity. It is through the hunt that he becomes a man. Among the Inupiat, the unwritten laws of survival and harmony depend not on how much one gathers and keeps for himself. A hunter's skill is measured by how much he gives away to those in need.

Roy Ahmaogak was one who was known among the Inupiat of Barrow (Roy's home village) and surrounding villages as an expert hunter. In response to the unwritten Inupiat law, he was admired for what he gave away. But God had planned for Roy to give away more than meat. And just as it is Inupiatun to have a hunting partner to stand beside you and share in your struggles for survival, so, too, Roy was to have a partner, only he wasn't to be Inupiat.

1

Ice Island

The wind, sharp and cold, came out of the northwest off the Beaufort Sea, across fifty miles of pack ice, stinging the tiny Inupiat settlement (about seventy-five miles east of Barrow, Alaska) with a chill factor of minus forty degrees. Outside Roy Ahmaogak's single-story wooden frame shack, his sled dogs—big Alaskan malamutes and Siberian huskies—slept curled up, head buried in flank, on the windward side of a hard packed snowdrift.

The November wind scarcely troubled these remarkable animals with their double insulated coats of fur. And for Roy Ahmaogak and the two or three extended families who made up the small community, the wind, especially since it was from the north, was a good sign. It meant the pack ice was safe for sealing or hunting polar bear or whatever else they found.

About as soon as an Inupiat boy begins to test his skill with the harpoon or comes to understand he must walk softly on the ice lest the seals he hunts hear him, he learns about wind. It is the wind, he is told, that controls the movement of the ice. Wind from the east or south pushes the ice pack off shore, but a northerly or westerly wind forces and holds the ice floes into shore. In all the stories the young people hear, especially stories told during the time of the long polar darkness (late-November to mid-January), there are always tales about hunters being trapped out on the ice pack. And the most fearsome are those about hunters who find themselves on an ice floe that has broken away from the main body of ice and are carried out to sea by a strong east wind.

But today was different. The wind was right, and in true Inupiat fashion of preparing a son for manhood by introducing him to the techniques of hunting, Roy decided his teenage son Waldo and he should go sealing. After a well fortified breakfast of tea, seal meat, and blubber, Roy and Waldo began to load up the family's basket sled. It was just to be an overnight trip, and trusting they would live off the animals they caught, Roy took only enough food for a day.

In every way, Roy Ahmaogak was Inupiat. To be outdoors and feel the cold wind on his face and to share in the high drama of a dog team going wild over the discovery of a seal's breathing hole, and to pit himself against the sovereignty of winter and such noble quarry as the Arctic animals, was to him the essence of life.

Then in 1920 at age twenty-two, a month after his second marriage to Isobel Manaluurak (Roy's first wife Alice died of tuberculosis), Roy was challenged with another reality beyond the hunt. He was assigned by the U.S. Government to take a census along 400 miles of coastal tundra between Barrow and the boundary of Alaska and Canada at a place with a four-foot marker called Demarcation Point.

It was on this trip, a trip he called his honeymoon,

that Roy discovered the Inupiat were hungry for more than boiled meat. Wrote Roy:

> When I first arrived in a village or trading post or small camp, I took a census of each one. Afterward I would read from my English Bible and translate orally into Inupiatun. In every camp it was the same. Everyone showed eager interest in the Word of God.
>
> When we arrived at Demarcation Point, I stood in front of the marker with one foot in Canada and the other in Alaska. I was happy and proud that the census was completed. But in another way, God seemed to tell me that I was to begin a new job. By his grace, God had placed in my heart a desire to put the Word of God into our own Inupiatun language.

While God had planted a seed in Roy's heart and mind, it was just a seed. Roy wasn't yet ready to deal with the implications of what was required to accomplish such a task. For the next seven or eight years, Roy eagerly and willingly juggled his hunting with his ecclesiastical and civic duties. As the first and youngest Eskimo to be ordained an elder in the Barrow Presbyterian Church, Roy taught Sunday School, sang in the choir, organized young people's activities, and conducted preaching missions with medical missionary Dr. Henry E. Greist. In this capacity, Roy acted as Dr. Greist's interpreter. And in June 1923, Roy, with Dr. Greist's help, organized the Wainwright Presbyterian Church.

Clearly Roy had an unusual talent and Dr. Greist began urging Roy to come under the care of the Presbytery and pursue a course of seminary study. But the more Dr. Greist urged, the more Roy resisted, until finally Roy gathered up his family and moved east of Barrow to a riverbank near Barter Island, about halfway to Demarcation Point.

For better than four years, Roy and his family lived in a settlement of not more than one or two families. Many of the dwellings were nothing more than one-room dome huts framed with whale bone and drift-wood, then covered with tundra sod. The semi-nomadic life-style of the Inupiat demanded that all hunting families have several such huts scattered all along the coast or wherever families camped out in search of their illusive quarry.

While Roy spent his days with what had always given him joy, the hunt wasn't quite as sweet as it once was. But Roy was stubborn, and in his self-imposed exile, clung to the belief that his life's destiny was to be a hunter. Then one cold day in November on a seal hunting trip with his teenage son Waldo, God, in a dramatic way, reminded Roy that his assigned destiny was to be more than trapping fox or stalking seal. Rather, Roy was to share, not meat, but the Bread of Life with the Inupiat.

Quickly and skillfully, Roy positioned each of his eleven dogs into their walrus hide harnesses with an ease that belied the difficulty of the task—eleven fifty- to sixty-pound dogs who squirmed, wiggled, and barked with an eager anticipation of the hunt.

The dogs weren't the only ones who were excited. The departure or arrival of a sled with dogs barking and choking as they tugged at their harnesses always awakened an Inupiat community with hope of fresh meat and news of friends and family.

The plan for the Ahmaogak family that day was simple. Roy's wife Isobel and their daughters, Alice and Elizabeth, would do the traditional woman's task—fishing. After fishing for tomcod through the offshore ice, they would go inland to fish the nearby lake (also through the ice) for trout, white fish, and Arctic char. The men, as if obeying the same migratory impulse as the animals they intended to harvest, pushed out onto the sea ice that had fastened itself to the shore. Isobel watched until the excited dogs pulled her husband and son out of sight, then gathered up her ice chisel, fish lines, and a few supplies, and called to her daughters to come and go fishing.

After their initial burst of eagerness to be about the business of hunting, the dogs quickly settled down to a "dog trot" whenever the ice was smooth and free of pressure ridges and ice hummocks. These smooth patches alternated with high pressure ridges caused by current, wind, waves, and the constant grinding and movement of the polar ice, some of them forming blocks of ice more than forty feet high.

One of Roy's reasons for suggesting he and Waldo go sealing on this particular day was the sky map he had seen about five miles offshore. A lead, or open water, is marked by a band of black clouds on the horizon (this is commonly called a sky map), and while Roy was expert in harvesting seals through their breathing holes in the ice, hunting off an open lead was a great deal easier. Besides, seals abandon their breathing holes in favor of an open water lead.

About a mile from shore, Roy and Waldo began to encounter excessively large pressure ridges that forced them into a long circuitous route to the lead. Finally, after a long hard trek, they reached the lead. The low circling sun had long since given way to the pale light of the moon. In the old days, Roy's grandparents and other hunters would have welcomed the bright soft light of the moon as a sign of good fortune. Roy didn't particularly believe in such old tales, but later, when Roy shared his harvest of four seals taken by the reflective light of the moon, the older people raised their eyebrows as if to say, "I told you so."

After shooting each seal, Roy retrieved them with

his *manak*. This was a pear-shaped wooden ball with several large hooks set on its surface. Expertly Roy threw the ball over the seal he had shot and carefully drew the barbed drag over it and pulled it to the edge of the ice. Roy had also taken his fourteen-foot skin kayak, dragged along behind the dog sled on its own small sled, to be used for hunting and retrieving the seal if the *manak* wouldn't reach. Fortunately it did, and he quickly turned his attention from seal hunting to setting up camp.

Like a well-rehearsed drill team, and without a word of instruction from Roy, Waldo and he began to pitch camp. From out of the dog sled, Roy unloaded his hunting box, a most important piece of equipment for an Inupiat hunter. One of the first items he reached for was his *pana* or snow knife. This was a single piece of caribou antler fashioned with an indented handle and a curved blade. Next came the snow shovel that Roy handed to Waldo. This was also made from an antler frame to which a piece of sealskin had been fastened with sinew. And lastly, he took out his snow probe. This, too, was made from antler and was about three feet long with an egg-shaped ferrule at one end and a small handle at the other.

With the snow probe, Roy pushed through the outer layer of soft snow to find a layer hard enough for snow blocks. And happily after their long and exhausting journey and seal harvesting, Roy found the exact density from which to cut his blocks.

Waldo removed the light snow with the shovel, and Roy, with his snow knife, began to cut out the rectangular block. Each was about twenty inches wide to about twenty-five inches long by about four inches thick. After cutting several such blocks, he set them on end sloping in toward the center and filled the cracks with loose snow.

Had he planned to stay on the ice for several days, he would have completed the igloo with a roof of snow blocks. Since they were tired, he took a large square of white tarpaulin from the sled and spread it over the snow block walls. Next, he securely tied the guy ropes to some nearby blocks of ice. The guy ropes were, in fact, not rope at all but rawhide from a bearded seal cut in a continuous inch-wide circle.

After Roy cut a two- to three-foot entrance hole into the snow house, Waldo made a raised sleeping counter. Then while Roy lit the lantern and got the Primus stove going to melt the blue ice★ for tea, Waldo dragged in a layer of caribou skins as insulation from the ice floor. After boiling some seal meat, drinking their hot tea, and feeding the dogs, Roy and Waldo fell instantly asleep. It should have been a long sleep to refresh them for all they had yet to do, but it wasn't. About 3:00 A.M. Roy suddenly awakened to an erratic fluttering of the canvas roof.

To the native as well as the uninitiated, the Arctic often appears an eerie, frightening place. Without warning, fogbanks can sweep in across the cold ice pack bringing zero visibility. And within a few hours, a "warm" dead calm day or night can be changed into one filled with a violent wind and blinding blizzard. And that was happening now!

It wasn't so much that the force of the gale was driving waves across the open lead and crashing up on top of the ice, or that the swirling mass of wind-driven snow was making visibility beyond a few feet impossible. What troubled Roy was the wind. It had shifted around and was now blowing from the east! And when he checked his compass and noticed the direction of the

★Old ice has a blue tinge to it and has the characteristic of losing most of its salinity and is thus suitable for drinking.

needle shift while he was standing still, his worst fears were realized. He and his son were in the middle of a huge ice island that had broken away from the shore ice and they were now drifting toward open sea!

Back on shore, Roy's wife and daughters were excited over an extremely good catch of fish. For the first few hours after Roy and Waldo left, the women chiseled holes in the shore ice and with a simple length of string suspending a small hook that they jerked up and down every now and then, caught over 300 six- to eight-inch tomcod.

After caching their fish in a rough hole cut into the permafrost of the tundra, Isobel and the girls moved inland away from the shore to a nearby lake. And there the fishing was every bit as exciting as on the edge of the Beaufort Sea.

About a hundred yards from the edge of the lake, Isobel knelt down and cupped her hands around her eyes as she peered through the ice. And then she spotted them, trout and grayling, swimming back and forth in their tranquil world of lake-bottom weeds. That tranquility, however, was soon to end. With deftness born from years of experience, Isobel took her ice chisel and with amazing speed and precision began to cut a twelve-inch hole through four feet of ice. Every few minutes she stopped and one of the girls with a bone ladle scooped the ice chips from the hole. When she finally chopped through the ice and water came up to the surface, one of the daughters carefully scooped away the remaining ice chips and slush.

Next, Isobel spread out a caribou skin, knelt down, and began a centuries-old practice of fishing through the ice with a decoy and three-pronged harpoon. The decoy was a piece of ivory carved into the shape of a small fish. This was weighted with a piece of soapstone and let down through the hole in the ice. When the fish, lured by the bobbing ivory decoy, swam by to investigate, Isobel gently lowered the harpoon into the hole and at the precise moment, speared the fish. The girls took part in this unique method of ice fishing as well. On and on they continued. Then tired and hungry and with their happy burden of fish, Isobel and her daughters made their way back to their ice cell cache and warm hut. There they intended to sleep and refresh themselves and fish yet another lake. But when they returned to their hut that stood on the edge of the Beaufort Sea, Isobel was horror-struck. The pack ice was gone! Just gray-black water lapped onto the black gravel shore. The wind, in concert with the offshore current and tide, had wrenched the pack ice clean from the grounded shore ice and pushed the huge mass out to sea.

Immediately Isobel understood the dire implications of what had happened. To hide the tears from her children and ease the heartbreak that tore in her breast, she clutched a mittened hand over her mouth. Somewhere out beyond the horizon on a floating ice island was her husband and son. Isobel knew that under its own creaking, grinding weight and with the help of wind and buffeting waves, the ice island would soon be broken up into digestible chunks and swallowed up forever by the eternal sea. In vain she searched the horizon for telltale signs of a sky map. But there was no contrastive reflection in the sky, only a uniform slate gray color clear out to the horizon. Numb with the finality of the evidence before her, Isobel could do nothing but pray and wait.

Unaware of the pain his wife was experiencing on shore, Roy quickly broke camp and for a time decided to keep the awful secret to himself. This decision to spare his son the uneasy anxiety sprang from the true essence and inner character of Roy Ahmaogak. It is very Eskimo, indeed very Inupiat, to hold one's self in reserve and be your own man. To have successfully survived the harsh polar environment for so many centuries demands a people marked by aggressive bravery and courage, as when they pit themselves against a fifty-ton bowhead whale or match one-on-one with a raging polar bear.

There is yet a further but less obvious reason for the survival of the Inupiat. It is their basic philosophy that they exist without chiefs. Decisions as to when to hunt and other such matters involve long discussions among adult hunters where everyone fully expresses his opinion. There are those who are known as thinkers, usually older men who have great influence by virtue of their age. But there are occasionally those who, while not old, command great respect by virtue of their ability to hunt *and* think. Roy Ahmaogak was one of these.

Like so many Inupiat, Roy's natural father was a nineteenth-century whaler. To this day, many Inupiat carry with pride a mixture of Scottish or Basque or Yankee, or as in Roy's case, Portuguese blood that has been mixed with their Inupiat mother's blood. Unlike many other cultures, to extend the kinship circle by adoption is a highly developed practice. No distinction is made by adoptive parents or the community between natural children and those born out of wedlock or of mixed blood.

Roy's birth in 1898 was remembered for two important events: one was the fawning of the caribou that spring; the other was a severe epidemic of measles that killed scores of children and adults in Barrow. Remarkably, Roy and his parents escaped this and other scourges of diptheria, influenza, and smallpox that had been introduced to the Inupiat by marauding whalers.

One reason may have been because, at the time, the Ahmaogaks lived on a spit of land about four miles east of Barrow. There is a special name given to those who live on this bare, narrow finger of tundra that juts into the Arctic Ocean—*Nuvugsmiut,* people of the point.

From the beginning, Roy's mother, a strong purposeful woman, perceived Roy to have a destiny beyond that of hunter and provider for his family. Introduced to Christianity by Presbyterian missions in Alaska,★ Roy's mother and adoptive father became first generation followers of Jesus Christ. Thus with her spiritual mind and new understanding of options open to her, Roy's mother began to prepare her son for his future ministry. She saw to it that he learned to read and write English and that he received all instruction open to him from the local Presbyterian church. If the Inupiat people in Barrow were to come to terms with and transcend the inroads of the white man's presence in the north, she knew her son would have to become educated. There was no school at the point so Roy was enrolled in school at Barrow and each day trudged four miles in and four miles back along the edge of the cold Arctic Ocean. If school was in session when it came time to follow the migratory animals, Roy stayed with friends. Nothing was to interfere with his schooling. And nothing did. Once the pattern for schooling was set, Roy accepted it almost without question, and he did indeed become educated. Further, he displayed what his

★To answer those who accuse Christian missions as disruptive of culture, the evidence shows that Inupiat Christians retained their culture as shown in the continuance of the hunt, dances, and other cultural events that mark them as Inupiat. To be Christians, as Roy's parents and many others experienced, is to be persons who after being introduced to Jesus Christ, trust Him as Redeemer and Lord and by faith try to exhibit in their daily lives conduct that brings honor to Him.

mother knew was there from the beginning—a compassionate and understanding desire to help his fellow Inupiat.

But then came the invitation from Dr. Greist, an invitation, interpreted by Roy, to take him away from all that was meaningful and comfortable. And to escape the pressure that had built over several years, Roy fled to an isolated fish camp on the Beaufort Sea. The warm glow of being among friends involved in the hunt was an important extension of his manhood and he didn't want to relinquish it. Besides, the white Arctic fox, along with polar bear and seal skins, provided him with a good cash flow.

Twelve hours had now passed since Roy and Waldo first set out on their seal hunting expedition. Then the wind had been their friend, holding the ice floes into shore. Now in a short span of time, the wind had changed into a formidable foe. It took less than ten minutes for Roy and Waldo to pack their equipment into the sled, load up the seals, lash down the load, and call for the dogs to head for shore. And here Roy ran into his first obstacle. Under normal circumstances, the dogs would have been only too eager to be off and running. But now they wouldn't or couldn't face the violent offshore wind. Understanding the dogs' dilemma, Roy quickly tied a rawhide line around the neck of the lead dog. Then draping the other end over his shoulder and with both hands tugging on the line, Roy bent himself into the wind.

Thus Roy and Waldo began to enact an odyssey as old as the first Inupiat who, when wanting something to eat, went hunting for it. It was a classic confrontation—man against nature. And from the way it began, there seemed to be no contest. Nature, with all her fury, would most certainly be the victor. Except man, this man, had what nature couldn't reckon with—an indomitable spirit.

Hour after hour, the dogs with lowered tails were led over the ice by two solitary figures, who, without speaking, pressed themselves in the direction of the wind. And the wind, as if fearing to lose the confrontation, sent swirling eddies of powdered snow into the eyes of men and dogs. Wisely, Roy knew how quickly the cold would overcome them if he, Waldo, and the dogs didn't take time to rest and eat. About every hour or so, when there was a lull in the storm or when they found a large snowbank or ice hummock for protection, they stopped to rest. It was important for the dogs as well as themselves to preserve their energy as much as possible. And while Roy boiled water for tea on the Primus stove, Waldo cut off liberal chunks of raw seal meat. Contrary to common belief, the Inupiat when given the choice prefer to boil their meat rather than eat it raw. But here Roy and Waldo didn't have a choice. As it was, they were running out of fuel for their Primus stove.

About midday, Roy and Waldo were pleasantly surprised to be overtaken on the ice by two other Inupiat hunters. In true Inupiat fashion, Roy was finding his direction with the help of his adversary, the wind. He could tell the wind's direction by the way the snow was drifting. The high part of the drift is always away from the wind where the eddy forms. Thus Roy was able to guide himself by the wind's plowed furrows. And because the other two men were Inupiat hunters, they, like Roy, understood the patterns and silent language of snow and wind. And they understood the silent language of sled tracks. By carefully observing these tracks in the snow, they could tell when they were made, how many dogs there were, and if the sled was loaded or empty. And when they came across Roy and Waldo's tracks, they knew what direction to take.

For the remainder of the day, the small group encouraged each other in the storm and walked on toward the shore. Late in the afternoon, they reached the landward edge of the ice island and found what Roy had feared—open sea. One of the hunters suggested they turn eastward toward where he thought there would be land. But after walking a short distance, the force of the gale became so intense Roy suggested they stop beside a large snowbank and dig in.

And dig in was the appropriate word. To build a snow house was out of the question. The swirling snow made it impossible to see beyond the lead dog on the team. When Roy tried to cut a few snow blocks to act as a screen against the wind, they blew out of his hands.

The dogs knew they weren't going anywhere. To conserve heat, they curled up into as tight a ball as possible and let the snow drift into their fur. Instinctively the dogs knew this would help keep them warm. Following the dogs' example, Roy took the tarpaulin and after digging out a sheltering hole in the snow, covered Waldo, the two men, and himself. There they stayed for three solid days.

Three days with nothing to eat but raw seal meat.

Three days without a fire.

Three days of relentless wind that drove its cold icy fingers through their wet furs to the very marrow of their bones.

Three days of deep anxiety when at any moment they knew the heaving, creaking ice might break up beneath them.

And it was also three days of intense soul searching. As the hours passed and Roy prayed for their desperate situation on the floating ice island, it suddenly came to him that he was behaving like Jonah. All his life he had responded to the Lord's direction, except in this case. He began to realize he was running away from the responsibility and ministry of providing Scripture for the Inupiat people. And the reason he was running was because a translation project would demand a drastic reduction in the amount of time he would be able to spend hunting.

As he reasoned with himself, he began to understand that there comes a moment of responsibility when the servant of God must choose between serving himself or his Lord; a time when one must face the difficult task of examining one's motives. And as if to confirm this, a verse of Scripture flashed into his mind: "I beseech you therefore, brethren, by the mercies of God, that ye present your bodies a living sacrifice, holy, acceptable unto God, which is your reasonable service" (Romans 12:1).

That you present your bodies. That you present your bodies. That you present your bodies. Over and over the words tumbled into Roy's mind. And then it came to him just as clearly as if the Lord himself had spoken it. *"This is My body given for you, and I want your body."* That was that. Roy knew what he had to do and was in that instant prepared to do it, except that he was still afloat on a large chunk of ice somewhere in the Beaufort Sea!

It was also at that moment a second verse of Scripture came into his mind—a verse he had learned in Sunday School from 1 Peter 5:7: "Casting all your care upon him for he careth for you."

Immediately Roy claimed the verse and there was a confirming sense of well-being that they were all going to get off the ice island safely. Later, when Roy finally told the others of their dilemma, they did not respond with curses about their bad luck or fate, or with cries against the hopelessness of their situation. Rather, they listened with great care and received the support and encouragement of Roy's reminder that the God whom they worshipped could cause the winds to change and push them back to shore.

And that's exactly what happened. The easterly wind that had pushed the ice floe out to sea, blew itself out and the stronger northwesterly wind picked up and began pushing them back toward shore. It took exactly a week for the ice island to reach a point where the men could drive their sleds off the ice onto solid land, a week of drifting that took them almost eighty miles from where Roy waved good-bye to his wife and daughters as they stood beside their hut.

Relieved and grateful to God for getting them back safely to shore, Roy and the others started back toward the hunting camp. Their ordeal was over, but for Roy, this was the beginning of a new and in many ways more exciting adventure than being cast adrift on an ice island. God had commanded his attention for the work He had assigned him. As yet Roy didn't know that translating the New Testament for the Inupiat was to be a team effort. He fully expected the burden to be his alone. And in 1946, Don Webster, the young man chosen by God to be Roy's partner, had not the slightest notion or interest in ever serving God in this way. In fact, this young Canadian from Pentanguishene, Ontario, was doing what Roy had been doing—running away.

2

Nothing Makes Sense in Isolation

"If you were an Eskimo, you would wear two fur parkas. These would be made from seal or caribou skin depending on what you were doing. Eskimos use different skins for their different activities like hunting, running a dog team, and so on. Seal skin is stronger, but the hollow hair of the caribou makes for ideal insulation against extreme cold. One of the furs would be turned to the inside against your skin; the other would have the fur facing outside. You would have a hood to cover your head and it would be trimmed with wolf or wolverine fur. There are many Eskimo language groups here in Canada and Alaska and each may call the outer parka by a different name. One group calls this outer parka *atigi*. Let's all try to pronounce this interesting word together: *a-ti-gi*. Good! You sound just like the Eskimo people I used to work with in the Northwest Territories."

The speaker was an Anglican minister who had been a missionary among the Eskimos of Northern Canada and was addressing a congregation in a small

Anglican church in Pentanguishene, Ontario. In 1946, this rural community of approximately 5000 people eighty miles northwest of Toronto was almost eighty percent French-speaking Catholics.

In the midst of this large French-Catholic presence, Miss Magnus, a local elementary school teacher, maintained a strong, effective evangelistic witness among the children of her school through a Bible club program. Many of these young people, after being introduced to Jesus Christ as Savior, came into a living faith. Don Webster was one of these. Actually, it was Don's older brother who first responded and in turn led Don into faith—not a growing faith, but a faith nonetheless. It was to be a faith that would one day be fanned into a glowing flame of enthusiasm, growth, and service.

Don was an eight-year-old choir boy in the Anglican church when he responded to his brother's witness. Now eight years later at sixteen, Don was listening to this Anglican minister talk about something that captivated his attention almost as much as his all-consuming passion of playing goalie on the high school hockey team. What enthralled him was that a people, not so terribly far from his front door, spoke a language different from English and French and lived a life style different from his.

More of a pragmatic realist than a poetic dreamer, young Don Webster's goals were to finish high school as quickly as possible, learn to fly a plane, play professional hockey, or become a truck driver. Yet deep within this young man was a latent giftedness—a giftedness for languages, and perhaps more important, a giftedness to interact empathetically with all kinds of people. Completely unaware of his own talent and not understanding why this speaker's use of the Eskimo language intrigued him, Don listened with rapt attention.

"In most cases, the Eskimos are among the friendliest people on earth," continued the minister, "but they do have customs that seem strange to us here in Pentan-guishene. For example, nothing seems to give them as much joy as welcoming visitors. Eskimos live in iso-lated communities of two or three extended families or in slightly larger communities and are always hungry for news of what's happening in other settlements. Therefore, when a visitor arrives at a small settlement, he is generally given what they call a 'mug up.' This is usually a big cup of thick hot soup, hard biscuits, and as much tea as he can drink. The fun comes, after telling all the news and giving greetings from friends, when an Eskimo gives forth a happy regurgitating belch. At that point everyone laughs and applauds, not by hand-clapping, but in Eskimo fashion by a long drawn out 'eh-eh-eh.'

"To belch in public is quite against what we would consider proper etiquette. But do you know we do something that is every bit as unpleasant in the eyes of the Eskimo, and I might add, in the eyes of God? Prov-erbs tells us that God hates pride and arrogance and those who boast and exalt one another. The Eskimo never exalts himself. Further he finds those who do most distasteful. Like God, the Eskimo is more in-terested in a man's character than his accomplish-ments."

Between his sixteenth year in 1946, and his gradua-tion from high school in 1948 at eighteen, Don's out-ward actions were marked with the routine of normal high school activities. In his senior year, he was captain of the Cadet Corps and student council president, yet these activities belied the torrent of emotional conflicts he was experiencing.

After graduation, many of Don's friends automati-cally entered the work force they intended to pursue as their lifetime careers. Others, with the same direction and purpose, went on to higher education. Don, on the other hand, was "fed up with school" and left home to become a truck driver in Toronto, the only boyhood dream that seemed an attainable option. Actually, before his graduation, he had been given a fourth career possibility.

Spotting him in the back pew one Sunday evening, Don's Anglican minister deliberately cornered him before he slipped out of the service. "You know, Don, I've been observing you over these past months, and I've wanted to speak to you about something you may never have thought about. You have a natural gift for leadership. You speak well before an audience, you're enthusiastic, and you have an interest in the church. I wonder, have you ever considered that God may be leading you into the ministry?"

That moment was surprisingly electric. Down deep in his soul, something snapped. It was a kind of instantaneous spark of recognition, a feeling of "yes, that's exactly what I should be doing with my life." But just as quickly as this beguiling notion beamed into his consciousness, there came a hard slam of another reality: "I don't want what such a decision would demand of me."

Always polite toward his elders, Don asked a few appropriate questions, all the while knowing that his natural effervescence demanded a more exciting career, and the minister closed the conversation by saying something about how God has given each person certain gifts that should, as part of good stewardship, be given back to the body of Christ as a service of love.

Don hadn't fully understood the deep implications of that conversation. All he knew, as he lay on his swayback bed in his tiny room on Spadina Avenue in downtown Toronto, was that after six weeks of driving a truck and eating in greasy spoon restaurants, he was more depressed than he thought he ever could be.

Alone in the emptiness of his own confusion, bored with truck driving, and never for a moment admitting to himself that he might be running away from God, Don decided to return to his hometown and enter grade thirteen (equivalent to first-year university but usually held on the local high school campus). However, he entered school two weeks after it started and was immediately frustrated with how little he understood and how far the class had advanced. After one day, he phoned the school principal and told him he was leaving school to join the air force. Years later Don was to recall that moment as being the lowest in his life.

If Don felt compelled to join the air force during the days when he couldn't get his mind to focus on school work, he wasn't quite as confident when the moment actually arrived. After hitchhiking into Toronto, he walked up and down in front of the air force recruiting office for almost an hour. Finally with a "what's there to lose" attitude, he grasped the handle of the door, opened it, and presented himself for service with the Royal Canadian Air Force for five full years.

That was September, 1948. For the next two years until October 1950, Don lived, as he himself describes it, as a person with "one foot in heaven and the other in hell." It wasn't that he didn't know who God was. He did. But by his attitude and chosen life style he was saying, "I'll come to You, Lord, only when I need You. I want You as an insurance policy tucked away in a safety deposit box in case I ever need help. But until that moment comes, just keep out of my way and let me live my own life the way I want to live it."

What Don didn't understand about God was how deeply He loves His children and that His primary reason for creating men and women is for fellowship. He may have understood that God became his friend through Jesus Christ, but he was so intent on living his life by his own wits, he had forgotten. Don surely had forgotten the stories in the Bible that describe God as the One who takes the initiative in restoring fellowship that has been interrupted through self-will, or indifference, or whatever has displaced a once warm, loving, and responding relationship with the Heavenly Father.

Turning points often come in unexpected ways, and on a crisp October Sunday night, Don experienced one of the most dramatic reawakenings of his life. Of that Sunday evening, he recalls the details as if it happened yesterday.

I was stationed at St. Hubert military base outside Montreal. It had been a long pointless kind of Sunday with boring conversation and nothing to do. In the late afternoon, for reasons I didn't fully understand (except that down deep inside I felt I should be living a different kind of life), I decided to go to church. I had been to Peoples Church in Montreal before and knew it to be warm and enthusiastic, and even though I had to take two busses and a streetcar for an hour's ride there and back, I decided to go.

The speaker's name was Bob Cook, an energetic man who read two passages of Scripture that immediately ripped me apart. The first was Genesis chapter six, verse three. It was a message of warning from God, and it seemed to be pointed directly at me. *"And the Lord said, My Spirit shall not always strive with man."*

As Bob Cook outlined the implications of this statement, I began to wonder if I had strayed over the mark, had sinned too much, had gone too deep for the Lord to take me back.

Then Bob read from Hebrews chapter twelve, verse twenty-nine: *"For God is a consuming fire."* I began to see that it was incompatible for me to claim Christ as my Friend and have the devil as my counselor.

As I look back, I probably interpreted those verses incorrectly, but I knew I was in danger of becoming hardened through the deceitfulness of my own pride. During the long altar call, I tried to convince the Lord and myself that I had done all that was necessary for salvation. I had repented of my sin, yet had no sense of assurance. Finally, in total desperation, I overcame my pride and indicated that I needed help by putting up my hand for prayer. At that instant, it was as though a burning sensation hit my chest and then slowly moved up to my head. I felt lightheaded, much like I had felt the night before when I was slightly intoxicated, but it was what I needed to assure me that God was receiving me into full fellowship. Never before had I experienced anything like this, and the evangelist made no reference to such a phenomenon. It just happened. As soon as I took a step toward the Lord in humility, admitting my total desperation and need, the Holy Spirit gave me the assurance I needed. I have since read of Finney, Moody, Billy Graham, and others having similar experiences, but at that time I knew nothing about this.

For the next several months, Don experienced a repetition of this emotion, though not in the fullness of that special night, and then it slowly faded away.

And so a change began to occur in Don Webster. The seed of faith that had lain dormant began to sprout and grow and bring new meaning, vitality, and purpose into his life.

One morning about six weeks after his spiritual renewal, Don walked into his mess hall and noticed the front page headline of the *Montreal Gazette:* AIRPLANE CRASHES IN SOUTH AMERICA, 23 MISSIONARIES KILLED. With alarm, sadness, and disbelief, Don read the details of how a DC-3, owned and operated by a mission enterprise known as New Tribes Mission, had slammed into a high mountain west of Maracaibo, Venezuela. Almost as if he had been knocked off balance, Don's mind flooded with doubts. "Missionaries, people of God trying to do good . . . dying . . . it doesn't make sense."

A couple of days later, still reeling from the anomaly of missionaries being killed while engaged in godly service, Don sought out his new friend, Steve Barney, from Peoples Church. (The night Don walked down the aisle of Peoples Church in response to a call of rededication, Steve volunteered to act as Don's counselor.)

Graciously, Steve had invited Don to the Wednesday night prayer meeting and volunteered to pick him up at the barracks. It was a critical time for Don. In his enthusiasm to share his new spiritual experience with his fellow air force buddies, he ran into a buzz saw of philosophical arguments he wasn't equipped to handle. Sensitive to Don's hazing by his buddies, Steve became a source of support and encouragement to Don in his new commitment.

Riding in from the barracks that night, Don began to question Steve about why God would allow his servants to die in such an accident. Don also questioned the role missions and missionaries played in the world. The only missionaries he knew about were Anglicans who worked with Eskimos in Northern Canada.

"I don't know too much about New Tribes Mission," said Steve, "only that they are one of a number of mission agencies who try to introduce native peoples to the Gospel of Jesus Christ. As for your question as to why God's servants suffer and die in accidents or in an untimely way, that's a hard one to answer. I suppose a smarter man than I am could give you chapter and verse, but I don't want to give you a pat answer to a difficult question. Just let me share a couple of thoughts.

"First, God never promises the Christian a life free from trials or suffering. In fact, part of the Christian's experience on earth is to be refined and made ready for heaven. And this refining has to come through all sorts of trials and testings. Jesus even said that no testing is pleasant, but afterward, when it is over, we will understand why we had to go through it. What the true child of God does know is that no matter what happens, God promises to be with him always.

"I guess that would be my answer. We just don't know why that plane crashed in Venezuela. It may have been pilot error. We do know it was overcast, and they couldn't reach the radio tower. But even in this terrible tragedy, we still have to trust God, just like Job did when everything was taken from him. Also we have the promise from Scripture that the Holy Spirit will help and give us power to face whatever problem confronts us."

For the time being, Steve's explanation about the paradox of suffering seemed to satisfy Don. But the question of responsibility for world mission began to loom large in his mind. Rather than coming to a place of rest over the plane accident, Don began to be dominated by a kind of depression.

It wasn't as much a depression as a growing conviction by the Holy Spirit that Don himself should become a missionary. At first he thought his depression was guilt feelings, but what did he have to feel guilty about? After all, he had experienced a profound spiritual awakening that had indeed changed his whole outlook and attitude toward life. Where once attending church and listening to someone preach from the Bible was drudgery, it was now the highest joy of his life.

Furthermore, he knew it couldn't be guilt before God because he believed implicitly in the promises from Scripture that anyone who faced his need of forgiveness and accepted Jesus Christ as Savior and Lord of his life is relieved of guilt. But still the depression remained as did the notion that God was leading him into some kind of mission work.

"It can't be possible that God wants me to become a missionary," reasoned Don. "I hardly know what a missionary is, or what he does, or what part of the world I should go to, or how much schooling I need . . . or anything!"

Always aware of His children's need for guidance, yet never willing to violate the human personality, God brought two tandem events into Don's life to help him choose his own course—the course God had designed for Don since the beginning of time.

The first event came to Don in the form of his hangar sergeant and a book the sergeant gave Don to read. It was a book about Eskimos!

"I've noticed you don't carouse around and drink with the boys like you used to," said the sergeant to Don one day.

"That's right, Sarge," said Don.

"I suppose it has something to do with this church I see you going to each Sunday and Wednesday."

"Yes, Sarge," said Don. "I—"

"No need to explain to me," interrupted the sergeant. "As long as my men keep out of trouble, I don't mind how they spend their time. Fact of the matter is, ever since I took part in the rescue mission back in 1946 of Canon John Turner, an Anglican missionary working up north among the Eskimos at Moffat Inlet, I've been kind of interested in the work of the church."

"What rescue mission was that?" asked Don.

"Canon Turner was accidentally shot in the head by a .22 rifle," said the sergeant. "The details are still rather sketchy. All I can remember is that an Eskimo had asked Turner to help him pull or drag in a large seal off the ice, about a 350 pounder. It was when Turner was helping the Eskimo that his gun accidentally discharged. The bullet struck the poor chap in the head. Didn't kill him though.

"The air force was called in to pick him up, and I with my crew was assigned to go and get him. The problem was, once we got to the Moffat Inlet, we had trouble with a magneto. And here I was without the proper timing equipment. Try timing a car without a timing light! Well, ours had to be taken apart and compared to its twin to bring it into correct timing and all this in sixty degrees below with the wind howling like a troup of banshees! All the while, this poor missionary was hovering between life and death and we were supposed to get him to a hospital in Winnipeg as fast as we could. We finally got the plane firing properly and flew to Winnipeg. The doctors operated, but he died a few weeks later. The story made national headlines, and we all got cited for saving the missionary. Anyway, it's all here in this little book. Thought you might like to read it."

Don did read the book, and afterward one night in particular stood out in his memory. As he took the hour-long, two-bus and streetcar ride into Peoples Church, he watched each person who got on or off. As he looked at them he thought, "There's a soul. He's either going to heaven or hell. Probably he's going to hell. They should be warned. And here I sit with the words of eternal life, and I'm not saying or doing anything about it." The longer he sat there, the deeper became his concern for the spiritual welfare of these people, so deep his depression intensified.

He was encouraged by the preaching message at church, but later that night, when he returned to the barracks, he was still depressed. Happily his roommate was out, and he thought perhaps if he prayed it would help. But even this didn't bring relief. Then, as he wondered why he was still so confused and depressed, the

Lord seemed to say, "Why don't you write a letter to New Tribes Mission and make yourself available for service?" But just as quickly as the thought came into Don's mind, he put it aside, and the depression remained.

Just a few short weeks before, Don, in a deliberate act of his will, had responded to an altar call in Peoples Church, thus saying to the world and himself, "I want to be different than I am." Such an act is called repentance. It was a thoughtful, courageous act that required Don to change his mind about God, about sin, and about himself. And this one bold step was the first of many such steps the Holy Spirit would prompt Don to take. Now, lying in a steel frame bed in a Canadian air force barracks, Don was once again being challenged.

The challenge was to translate his emotions of pity, concern, care, and compassion into positive action. Don knew if he was ever to get to sleep, he would have to resolve, this very night, the issue of his willingness to be a missionary. At last, after tossing and turning for better than an hour, Don decided to get up and write a letter to New Tribes Mission. "If I receive a positive response," Don thought, "I will try to buy my way out of the air force and become a missionary." It was a difficult decision, and he had a hard time admitting to himself that this is what he wanted to do, but after writing the letter, he knew intuitively that what he had done was right. He thanked the Lord for this assurance, popped back into bed, rolled over, and promptly fell asleep.

Almost by return mail Don received a firm invitation from New Tribes Mission for him to join their ranks for mission service, probably in Latin America. In keeping with his resolve to try and buy his way out of his remaining three years in the air force, Don wrote a letter to his commanding officer. Carefully Don explained his recent spiritual experience and outlined the reason why he wanted to be relieved from military duty.

The commanding officer's reply was immediate: "Request to pay for unfulfilled military service denied." Further, with the denial came orders for Don's squadron, one of the two special squadrons of F-86 Sabre jets, to be ferried to England as part of Canada's commitment to NATO. Without a second's hesitation, Don accepted his commanding officer's decision as the Lord's will. New Tribes would have to wait. What Don didn't or couldn't know was how important his two years in England would be to his future ministry.

Don's landing in England in November 1951 coincided with the defeat of Britain's Labor Party, the reinstatement of Winston Churchill as Prime Minister, and the devaluation of the British pound. While this devaluation meant extreme hardship for Britons, it was advantageous for those with Canadian or American dollars. One of these advantages for Don was his ability to buy a motorcycle.

Stationed in the village of North Luffenhan, ninety miles north of London, Don spent his free time exploring the countryside and experiencing the thrill of a cool bracing wind whipping around his head as he sped up and down the narrow country lanes. It was a happy time for Don. He was relatively free from anxiety; he had as much money as he needed, and perhaps because of his own English heritage inherited from his proper English mother, he fell in easily with the local gentry. Then one night the inevitable happened.

It was a dark and foggy night, and Don had taken another RAF fellow on back of his bike to a Youth for Christ rally. They were returning to the barracks when Don, traveling too fast, found himself in a hair-pin turn he couldn't negotiate. In an instant they were down, skidding toward a big oak tree. Don, in a reflex action to avoid hitting the tree, stuck out his foot. There was a sickening snap; it was a vertical break in his ankle. Then and there he decided to end his days as a motor bike rider.

After six weeks in a walking cast, Don traded his motorcycle for a pedal bike and began visiting a local Methodist chapel in the village of North Luffenhan.

It was a large parish with just two itinerant preachers to serve a variety of outlying chapels. Frequently laymen would officiate as preachers, and when Don began to attend the chapel regularly, the ruling elders invited him to preach for them. If there was one outstanding feature that characterized Don Webster then, as now, it was his healthy enthusiasm for spiritual values. The elders recognized this and wanted their congregation to be encouraged with Don's energy and fresh approach to the Scriptures. For almost two years Don served that chapel and others as their lay preacher whenever he was free from military duty. Of that moment in time, Don says he believes it was planned of God. "If I hadn't broken my ankle, I probably would never have settled down in one spot. And if I hadn't settled down and in a sense become landlocked, I probably never would have learned to preach."

It was important that Don learn to preach and gain pastoral experience because the very person Roy Ahmaogak was to request from the Summer Institute of Linguistics to be his helper was to be someone who knew how to preach and who was interested in pastoral duties. It was to be an abnormal request of the Institute since few of its membership are ever ordained or have an interest in the ecclesiastical functions of the church. Their job is to translate the New Testament for ethnic minorities without the Scriptures in their own language.

Of course, in 1952, Don had no idea that such a

man as Roy Ahmaogak even existed or that there was an organization dedicated to the translation of the Scriptures into ethnic languages. Furthermore, Don hadn't the faintest notion of where he would one day serve as a missionary or with what mission organization. In order for these seed thoughts to be planted and germinated in Don's mind, however, God had to get his attention. And one night in the basement of a church, God used a missions conference and a simple display of artifacts to once again capture Don's interest in Eskimos and becoming a missionary.

Don had never been to a missions conference. As he walked around to view the various mission displays, he was impressed with the variety of mission organizations and what they were doing for world evangelism. But there was one small exhibit that challenged him above all the rest. It was a simple display of white igloos and a few Eskimo artifacts resting on a white bed sheet. When Don saw the young man who represented the mission and understood he worked among Eskimos in the Arctic, something happened inside. There was a warm inner glow that confronted Don like the first time he heard about Eskimos from the Anglican missionary who came to his church in Pentanguishene and when he read the book from the sergeant. And although he didn't make a decision then and there, somehow down deep he knew that one day he would work among Eskimo people.

3

You're in Bloomfield, Not Barrow!

It hardly seemed possible, yet here he was—Roy
Ahmaogak standing before 3000 delegates and observers of the General Assembly of the United Presbyterian
Church assembled in Atlantic City, New Jersey, on
Wednesday night, May 27, 1946. Just twenty-five days
earlier, Roy, accompanied by seven well-wishers, left
his home in Barrow and traveled to the local airport via
dog sled. From there Roy flew to Fairbanks and then on
to a series of bedazzling hopscotch jumps across the
lower forty-eight to arrive in time to be introduced to
the General Assembly by Rev. Merlyn A. Chappel.

The trip to the General Assembly was one among a
series of firsts for Roy, now forty-eight years old. It was
the first time he had been outside his world of snow, ice,
fog, and tundra. Further, the population of Barrow in
1946 was just under 1500 inhabitants who all lived and
worked in single story buildings. Thus, when Roy
attended his first baseball game in New York, he wrote
with stunning simplicity, "It was the largest crowd I
had ever seen!"

Without any of the high-blown rhetoric or emotion of a first-time visitor to that great city, Roy wrote in a matter-of-fact way about visiting the Empire State Building and seeing the 8th Fleet on the Hudson River. Strangely absent from his diary was how he felt about his first ride in an elevator and a trip to the zoo. However, traveling companion Dr. Jackman provided the missing insight into that moment.

"For Roy to walk into our modern mechanized civilization at age forty-eight was a breathless experience. I shall never forget Roy's look of astonishment the first time the elevator took him down. And when we went to the zoo and Roy saw many of the animals mentioned in the Bible, like the camel, sheep, and lions, we all gained a new awareness of what it's like to see something for the first time when you have only read or heard about it. It was complete joy for us to be a part of Roy's first-time experiences."

Later when Roy visited Philadelphia, his words were still matter-of-fact and simple, but reading between the lines one could feel his profound sense of respect, awe, and humility when he wrote:

> Today I stood and touched the Liberty Bell. Saw City Hall and stood on the platform where Abe Lincoln stood to put up the flag on Independence Day.

Roy's spoken words were equally simple and direct. Yet there was a certain power to them, a power that came not from cleverly constructed syntax. Rather, the power came from within the man. Roy was a man without pretense, a man who never seemed to take himself too seriously. He was a man who, while not overly self-effacing, never brought attention to himself. "He was," said one colleague, "tremendously well-balanced."

This feeling of quiet confidence came partly from his own rich heritage and history as an Inupiat. But it also came from a clear mandate to be a minister to his own people, a mandate he believed God had given him during the ice island experience. And on that Wednesday night in Atlantic City when he was introduced to the General Assembly and was elected Elder-Commissioner, he, with his gentle humor and authentic spirit, endeared himself to the whole assembly. The ice island story held the Assembly on the edge of their seats. But it was Roy's final story that set heads nodding in knowing approval and respect for the Eskimo from Barrow.

After the ice island experience, Roy began to think seriously about the direction of his life and that of his nine children, all of whom were growing up without formal schooling. For the first time since leaving Barrow, Roy admitted to himself he had indeed been running away from God. And just as freely he admitted, with thankfulness, it was God who had intervened and allowed the wind to change and blow the ice floe back to shore without breaking up. Yet with all this evidence before him, Roy still wanted to know for sure he was truly being called of God. In spite of more than a four-year absence from the life and ministry of the Barrow church, Roy had always carried a burden for the spiritual well-being of his people. Nor had he forgotten how enthusiastic he had once felt about the notion of giving the Scriptures to the Inupiat in their own language. Therefore, after the example of Gideon's experience, Roy prayed and put out a fleece.

"Lord, if this conviction in my heart to return to Barrow and have my children educated and to surrender myself fully to Your cause is true, I will say nothing to anyone regarding this prayer or my past experiences. I will say nothing about this to the new minister (Rev.

Fred Klerekoper who had replaced Dr. Greist as the new missionary pastor of the Barrow church). But, dear Lord, if it is truly Your will that I should fully surrender to work for You full time, have the new minister, who doesn't know me or anything about how I used to interpret or any of my past involvement with the church, have him approach me on this matter."

It was a courageous prayer, a prayer that reflected Roy's willingness to suspend his preoccupation with hunting and to give himself in selfless service to God.

The ice island experience had occurred in November 1936. Shortly after that Roy moved his family to within approximately thirty-five miles of Barrow, about a day's journey for a good dog team. That spring, April 8, 1937, to be exact, Rev. Fred Klerekoper, on a pastoral dogsled trip to Demarcation Point, spent the first night on the trail at Roy's house. On the following morning, Fred and Roy, using Roy's dog team, started out together for Demarcation Point. The full details of how and why Roy decided then and there to accompany the new Presbyterian minister to Demarcation Point are lost. It is known, however, that after he observed Roy's natural ability as a leader and his facility in both English and Inupiatun, Fred asked if Roy would interpret his sermons. Roy said yes.

Another possible reason why Roy decided to go on this trip is that it is very Eskimo to take off on an adventure unexpectedly and without too much premeditation. And what an adventure it was. Penetrating cold, insufficient food, apprehension over direction, and the eerie feeling and quiet grandeur of being out on the icepack fifty miles from land as they moved toward their destination. But in the midst of all this were the people—warm friendly people who welcomed them and shared their small cluttered huts, food, and hot tea with the travelers.

In a way quite beyond Roy's expectation, God dramatically reminded him of his own trip to Demarcation Point sixteen years earlier. In all that time, little had changed. The Inupiat still hunted and fished as they had always done. There had been deaths and births, good times and bad, and the Inupiat still evidenced a hunger and desire for the Word of God in their own language. So much in evidence was this desire for an Inupiat translation of the Scriptures that the new minister decided he should take some practical and positive steps to bring this need into reality.

Rev. Fred Klerekoper knew such a gigantic undertaking as a New Testament translation would be more than he could handle by himself. He would need a helper, a teammate. He would need someone who could work as easily in English as in Inupiatun. He would need someone who knew Eskimo culture inside and out. He would need someone like Roy Ahmaogak.

Further, Fred knew that to assume such a task, he would need special training in linguistics. And if the team was to be truly effective, Roy would also need further training, both in linguistics and in theology. To realistically accomplish this, Roy would need financial help. Fred knew enough about Inupiat culture to understand that Roy would have to have money to buy food for his family if he was to ever leave the North Slope on a study program. He would arrange for Roy to receive a salary through the Presbyterian Board of National Missions.

Fred was totally unaware of all that God had been doing in Roy's life. He knew nothing of Roy's prayer and the fleece he had put out. And on the day Fred spoke to Roy about considering giving himself to the care of the Presbytery for training and full-time ministry, it all seemed too easy. Without any visible display of emotion, Roy, who months before had come to grips with allowing his feelings to override obedience to what God commanded, said, "Yes." In that moment, Roy realized God had answered his prayer.

To ready his new colleague for the responsibilities of the Barrow church during his absence to study linguistics with translation expert Dr. Eugene Nida★ at the Summer Institute of Linguistics (SIL), Fred took Roy under his tutelage. For a full year, 1938 to 1939, Roy worked side by side with the American missionary pastor. And in June 1940, when Fred and his family left Barrow for Sulphur Springs, Arkansas, and "Camp Wycliffe"† to study linguistics, Roy assumed the preaching responsibilities for the Barrow Church.

The following spring, Fred Klerekoper returned to Barrow eager to try out his linguistic wings. With Roy as his chief colleague, both set to work devising an Inupiat alphabet. For the next four years, they assumed a variety of responsibilities, and in their "spare" moments worked hard on trying to analyze the complex Inupiatun language.

True to Fred's word, Roy came under the care of the Presbytery and became a salaried worker for the Presbyterian Board of National Missions. Roy also found time to run the local co-op store where his fellow Inupiat came to trade their fox furs for staples and supplies. And as if he didn't have enough work to do, he also became a part-time school teacher. In 1942 the Bureau of Indian Affairs granted him a teaching certificate, this without the advantage of having attended high school or college.

★Dr. Nida, one of the world's foremost Bible translation experts, is currently the Executive Secretary of the American Bible Society in New York.

†Because of its spartan camp-like qualities, early members of Wycliffe Bible Translators referred to the place in Sulphur Springs where SIL was held as "Camp Wycliffe."

Then in 1945, Rev. Klerekoper left Alaska to assume a gospel ministry in Iran. This left the North Slope temporarily without a pastor, and many people assumed Roy would fill that vacancy. He, after all, had proven himself an able lay preacher during Fred's absence in both the Wainwright church he helped establish with Rev. Greist and the Barrow church. But under the Presbyterian form of church government, Roy could not assume permanent pastoral duties until he had been ordained. And he couldn't be ordained to the Presbyterian ministry until he had some theological training.

Those serving on the Board of National Missions were keenly aware not only of Roy's talent, love, and apparent fitness for the ministry, but also of the desire the Inupiat had for him to become their pastor. The Board was also impressed with Roy's interest and hard work in trying to provide the Scriptures for the Inupiat church. Thus it was decided that Roy, like Rev. Klerekoper, should spend a year in study, first at the Summer Institute of Linguistics with Dr. Nida, then in the fall at Bloomfield Seminary in New Jersey. Since the General Assembly was meeting that May, the Board felt it would be a helpful and important meeting for Roy to attend before going to SIL. As it turned out, it was a most helpful meeting for Roy, but more so perhaps for the delegates and observers to the General Assembly. Many of the people who met Roy Ahmaogak and heard his testimony that May evening in 1946 considered it to be one of the highlights of the convention.

Typically, Roy was quite unaware of how people perceived him. He was just himself, which is why so many people were blessed and encouraged by his life and testimony. And it would be the same when Roy began his linguistic studies.

Rev. Fred Klerekoper had studied his linguistics at Sulphur Springs, Arkansas. But now the Summer Institute of Linguistics was held at the University of Oklahoma at Norman, noted as much for its high summer humidity and fierce heat as it is for its famous football enthusiasm. For a man who heretofore hadn't experienced temperatures much above fifty degrees, trying to study in the high nineties and low hundreds with an equal amount of humidity was painful indeed.

In an effort to overcome some of this discomfort, Roy tried to keep cool by eating ice cream, the effects of which caused him to write the following entry in his diary:

July 6, 1946
Sunshine as always. Every day sweating (it is nice not to suffer from cold). Took sick in the night and suffered tummy ache. Did not sleep any during the night due to pain. Had to wake the doctor at 6:00 A.M. Was taken to the hospital about 10:30.

In an earlier entry in his diary, Roy had attributed the same pain to too much ice cream. Then it was just a "miserable day." On this occasion, however, Roy was hospitalized for two days. Finally on the day he was returned to class, Roy wrote:

July 9, 1946
Slept so soundly I almost overslept. Was the last one to come to breakfast table. Had a warm welcome from the whole school. Everyone clapped their hands when I showed up and it made me happy. Had a full breakfast. Lunch meal wasn't anything I wanted to eat, so didn't, just to be on the safe side.

If Roy played it safe with his diet after his hospitalization, he wasn't the least fearful about trying out new experiences, including swimming. While the Inupiat of the North Slope spend ninety percent of their hunting

experience in and around water, few if any in 1946 knew
how to swim. Two entries dated July 12 and 13 reveal a
childlike wonder into how Roy felt about his new experience.

> Nice day. It seems we never get a cloudy day here. Dr.
> Nida and I went swimming and he taught me how. Could
> float a little and swam a little after a fashion. He held me
> with one hand and made me swim. Enjoyed it very much.

> Hot again. Went swimming. Improved from yesterday's
> first try. Enjoyed it very much.

And by summer's end, Roy was swimming the
length of the pool with ease. At last he had found a way
to beat the heat. Sometimes good-natured staffers let
Roy cool off in the kitchen walk-in freezer. "It was,"
said Roy, "the most heavenly of all."

Of course not everything was fun and games at
SIL. Roy and John McIntosh, the affable Wycliffe translator with a twinkle in his eye, spent long hours each
day analyzing the Inupiatun language. Since this language was unwritten, one of their principal assignments
was to devise an alphabet. Rev. Klerekoper had done
some work on this, but more was needed.

After pulling together a phonemic alphabet, Roy
then tried his hand at a beginning translation of Mark's
Gospel and the Epistle to the Romans. Dr. Nida, the
energetic and scholarly translation technician, had both
the interest and experience to give Roy the help he
needed. And together the two men worked throughout
the long hot summer.

In addition to working on his own language projects, Roy assisted the beginning linguists by role playing. Pretending to speak only his native Inupiatun
language, Roy let the students use him in their experi-
mentation or testing of the language learning techniques

they were being taught in the classroom. Since this is a regular part of the SIL program, there were other ethnic peoples who, like Roy, took part in language learning demonstrations. One evening at a gathering for these ethnic peoples, Roy sang the hymn, "Alas and Did My Saviour Bleed." Later one of the men introduced himself to Roy.

"Mr. Ahmaogak," he said, "when you sang that hymn, it felt like a cool breeze suddenly came over me. You can tell I am blind and I can't see you, but I want to tell you that even though you are Eskimo and I am Indian, we are brothers."

Roy was a brother to all who knew and worked with him that summer of 1946. And when he left SIL on a train for Chicago, he experienced the bittersweet ache of saying good-bye to friends he knew he would in all probability never see again this side of heaven.

Roy's diary revealed the poignancy of that moment. It also revealed how deeply he felt about having to leave the swimming pool. Since that first day when Dr. Nida introduced Roy to the weightless joys of swimming, Roy noted this special pleasure in his diary. And on the several days his study load prevented him from getting into the pool, he noted this also. Roy recorded this disappointment with the same feelings a young man might express when he goes off to college for the first time and has to leave his dog behind.

After a reunion and visit of several days in Montecello, Indiana, with his former pastor and friend, Dr. Henry Greist, Roy once again boarded a train, this time for Bloomfield Seminary in Bloomfield, New Jersey.

Roy arrived in Bloomfield on September 15 before any of the other students. From the beginning of his experience there, his diary reveals, though never explicitly, that he was lonely indeed. All his life he had faced the high challenge of each hunting season with enthusi-

astic expectation and the shared camaraderie of his hunting mates. While there was no opportunity to display
his prowess as a hunter at SIL, there was the high
academic challenge. There were also people who loved
and cared with the same robust sense of high purpose he
had sensed on the whale hunt. At the seminary there
was, of course, his prescribed course of studies, and
these he accomplished without comment. He did, however, comment on his efforts to continue his translation
of Mark and Romans, and in the midst of all this was a
growing sadness.

Sept. 7, 1946
Went to church at my own choice to the First Presbyterian.
For most of the day I listened to several services and ser-
mons through the radio in my room.

Sept. 9, 1946
Spent most of the day in my room reading, writing, and
listening to the radio. The only time I run out is when I go
out for meals. It is sort of tiresome due to monotony.

Sept. 19, 1946
Nothing changed much. Did my regular routine—translating, going out to eat (alone) and listening to the radio. It
must be fall now because the leaves are falling, yet the
weather doesn't feel like it. Very different from Barrow's
fall.

Yet in spite of the sameness of each day and the
particular loneliness on weekends, even with his regular
church attendance, Roy did experience a few notable
moments. In late November he made his second trip to
New York and there had his first subway ride. He also
did what many have only wished they could do—visit
the Statue of Liberty and climb to the crown and look
out over that spectacular harbor and skyline.

Equally as exciting to Roy as visiting the great

symbol of freedom was to see a large group of people gain spiritual freedom as they came forward to accept Jesus Christ as personal Savior during an Old Fashioned Revival Hour crusade in Madison Square Garden. Roy was particularly impressed with the immense crowd. He noted that "20,000 people came and filled the Garden to capacity."

The excitement of New York, however, was quickly over, and Roy returned once again to the sedentary life of a theological student at Bloomfield. For a man used to the outdoors and the heady exhilaration of hard physical exercise, life at Bloomfield was akin to fishing in a goldfish pond when he literally had been used to tackling, with a simple hand-held harpoon, a thirty-ton bowhead whale.

Therefore, when Roy wrote that he and a professor went to the Y.M.C.A. for a swim, then returned to his room where he read and listened to the radio, only those who knew his background could capture his saddening spirit when he ended with, "It is quiet all the time."

But nothing in his diary quite caught Roy's cheerless, almost broken-hearted spirit as when he wrote on December 21, 1946:

> Christmas vacation begins this noon. Will be quite alone by nightfall when all have left for their respective homes.

Of course Roy wasn't altogether forgotten. Some friends did invite him to their home on Christmas Eve, and together they enjoyed a candlelight service. This was followed by a drive around the neighborhood to see the festive lights and then home for more caroling and Christmas goodies. On Christmas day, Roy enjoyed an old-fashioned Christmas dinner and the rich fellowship of Christian friends. It was all very wonderful, yet there lingered the rich memory of Christmases past when the village of Barrow met together, young and old, children and adults, men and women, for a full week of Christmas festivities. One can only surmise how Roy must have missed the warmth of an Inupiat Christmas festival, and when at the end of Christmas day he returned once again to the loneliness of his room, he began to remember.

He remembered how the Christmas celebrations evolved out of the activities that took place during the months of darkness. Traditionally, these were the months when people came together in deep community to play games and listen to storytellers. And an Eskimo story was not just a bedtime story. These were epic stories of brave hunters who saved the people from starvation during times of famine. They were stories of hunters getting lost on the ice (like Roy) and stories of hunters battling the mighty bowheads. So exciting were these stories that they took a month to relate, with several men telling different segments of the story.

Roy remembered all this, and he remembered how at Christmas the whole village gathered for a week of feasting and sharing their food. Good food like *ugruk* meat, caribou stew, cooked polar bear, frozen fish, duck, and *muktuk*. In his remembrance there were no individual trees in the homes; instead, there was a communal tree in the church, and each child received some small gift his parents had bought at the co-op store. And after the feasting there would be testimonies and songs and games. For the games the whole village would be divided into two teams using the most favorite names— "foxes" and "polar bears." And no matter your age, young or old, and no matter if you participated or not, each was assigned to a team. All knew they belonged, and all cheered appropriately in a spirit of friendly rivalry for their team.

There were informal games like the famous string figures. Mostly, however, the games centered around strength, endurance, and resourcefulness of the kind needed to live and survive in the Arctic. Games like a ten-mile round-trip foot race in minus thirty-five degrees. Or standing broad jumps (often across open leads). There was kick ball and games that required the men, with miniature bows and arrows, to shoot at small bits of wood strung from rafters. The targets were make-believe ptarmigans.

And not to be outdone, the women had their games. One of the famous games was attaching a piece of string around each other's ear and engaging in a mini-tug-of-war. The first one to yield lost the match. Other games included lifting weight by one's ear.

Perhaps the most famous and spectacular game of all (not counting the *nalukatak*—a blanket toss that marked the end of a successful whale season) was the Eskimo high kick where a man was required to jump with both feet together and touch an object level with his eyes and land back on his feet. Roy remembered all this and the times he himself had tried to perform this amazing test of agility.

And then Roy remembered the dances that climaxed the festival on New Year's Eve. Men in their finely worked and beautifully embroidered sealskin *mukluks* danced to the accompaniment of singers and tambourine-type drums made from seal or walrus intestine stretched taut over a wooden hoop and struck with a willow wand. Limited to men only, the dances were dramatic imitations of the game they hunted. There were standard steps everyone recognized, but depending on the skill and cleverness of the dancer, he could innovate and work out his own variations—and most, to the delight of the crowd, did just that.

But Roy wasn't in Barrow; he was in Bloomfield.

He reminded himself of something he had written at SIL when he was suffering through the fierce Oklahoma heat:

> These are warm days for me, but must take them as a good soldier. No complaining will do any good.

If ever a statement characterized a man, this deliberate choice not to complain was true of Roy Ahmaogak all his life. To survive the uncompromising weather and capriciousness of migratory animals meant you were continually faced with sets of choices—choices that demanded clear thinking and unemotional judgment. And no matter how devoid of community Roy felt the seminary was, he knew in order to survive the remainder of the academic year he would have to make a choice. The choice was not to allow whatever emptiness he was experiencing to overcome his commitment to accomplish what he knew God wanted him to do. Besides, it wasn't all that long until June when he would return to Barrow.

But Roy was not to return to Barrow. Instead he and his family would move ninety miles west of Barrow to the coastal village of Wainwright where at the age of forty-nine, he would become the first Eskimo to be ordained to the Presbyterian ministry. Further, he would become the pastor of the Olgonik (Wainwright) Presbyterian Church, the very church he and Dr. Greist had founded twenty-four years earlier.

4

The Metamorphosis

It was one of those fleeting glimpses captured on the fringe of one's vision. As Don turned from looking into his pigeon-hole mail box, a pair of outstandingly blue eyes caught his attention as she passed in the hall. "Who was that?" he mused. "How did I miss her at the orientation?" As Big Brother, he had been responsible for welcoming the freshman class and organizing the fun events of their orientation week.

The fall session at the London Bible Institute and Theological Seminary was nicely under way when this intriguing question gripped Don's attention. This began a secretive search. It wasn't long before he spotted them again and found that they belonged to a pretty young nurse. Her name was Thelma Cudney. His first impulse was to ask her for a date, but as a second-year seminarian, it didn't seem right to begin dating a freshman at the beginning of the term. Also, he had no idea what she was like. Was she the kind of person who would be willing to serve God cross-culturally? He didn't want to get involved with someone who was unprepared for the rigors of foreign service. Therefore, for two long years, he resisted his impulses to discover the personality behind those blue eyes.

It was easy to remain strangers. He was a seminarian; she was a lowly freshman Bible school student. He was popular and gregarious; she was quiet and timid. Then too, Thelma Cudney was a registered nurse, lived off campus, and worked many nights and most weekends to pay her tuition and expenses. So the one-way admiration continued. Or was it one way?

This was Autumn 1954, when the signature of the times for millions of Americans and Canadians was Joe Friday in the weekly radio series "Dragnet" saying, "All I want is the facts." It was also a time when television had come of age and the viewing public had been introduced to Edward R. Murrow's furrowed brow and velvet voice, and such notable programs as "Leave It to Beaver," "Ozzie and Harriet," and "Father Knows Best." And certainly in Don Webster's and Thelma Cudney's case, their Heavenly Father had indeed known best and led them independently by circuitous routes to attend the London Bible Institute (LBI) in London, Ontario.

A year earlier, in July 1953, Don, after a full five years in the Royal Canadian Air Force, had been honorably discharged. He was now free to pursue the strong inclinations he had felt several years before to serve God by acquainting a confused world with the healing love of Jesus Christ. Just where in the world this would be and through what mission vehicle, Don didn't yet know. At that moment the more important question was what school he should attend to prepare himself for this ministry.

Before his tour of duty in England, Don had been introduced by a friend to the notion of one day studying at Prairie Bible Institute (PBI) in Three Hills, Alberta. "PBI is a great school to train for the ministry," Don's friend had said. He had no quarrel with his friend's enthusiasm about PBI being a great place to train for the ministry. It was simply a question of old-fashioned Canadian practicality and frugality. After considering the distance from Pentanguishene, his home town, to Three Hills, Alberta, it simply made more sense to choose a school in his own province.

However, the decision for brown-haired Thelma Cudney from Galt, Ontario to attend LBI hadn't been quite so pragmatic. Thelma, with her three brothers, her devout Presbyterian mother, and not so devout father, lived on the outskirts of Galt, an uncomplicated 130-year-old textile mill town in eastern Ontario. Like the town, Thelma and her family were also uncomplicated. Thelma's father provided for his family by delivering ice in the winter and wood in the summer. This he did until refrigerators became popular and his company went bankrupt. Mr. Cudney then became a boiler-maker, a job he held until he retired.

Thelma's mother was the kind of woman who wore a white apron over a printed housedress and put up preserves to help stretch the family budget. She was also the kind of woman who saw to it that her only daughter said her nightly prayers and attended Sunday School regularly. And while the Cudney home was maintained in the manner of an ice man's wages during the early forties, it was a happy home with lively interaction between Thelma and her brothers.

Quite naturally Thelma's values and aspirations reflected the mood and tenure of her home and town. For as long as she could remember, Thelma entertained the notion of becoming a nurse. There was, however, one aspect of her vision that reached beyond the dream of nursing in an ordinary hospital. Her fancy was much more romantic: she felt a strong tug toward the North.

As a true daughter of Canada, she had grown up with stories of Canada's heroes, frontiersmen, explorers, soldiers, Indian warriors, and seamen. Men like Samuel de Champlain, often called the Father of Canada. Others like General James Wolfe, the Marquis de Montcalm, and Frontenac, who when asked to surrender Quebec replied, "I will answer to your General only by the mouth of my cannon!" And who didn't know about the brave Adam Dollard who at age twenty-five, with only sixteen men, fought the frightening Iroquois in a kind of Custer's last stand?

Every Canadian school child knew about Eskimos, fur traders, French Canadian canoemen, the Hudson Bay Company, Captain George Vancouver, Simon Fraser, and the remarkable Alexander Mackenzie who in 1789 unknowingly reached the Arctic Ocean after a perilous three-thousand-mile journey. When Thelma heard and read about these and other explorers, it seemed as if they were part of her own life experience. As a young girl, she lamented being born in a day when people crossed the prairies in speeding automobiles. She wished for the days of prairie schooners pulled by teams of plodding oxen. But Thelma grew up and became wiser and had to admit the forties and fifties did have some advantages over the 1800's. Yet, even during nurses' training, she clung to the dream of serving in some out-of-the-way northern outpost.

It may have been a fanciful dream, but the One who guides often does so through our desires, and from the beginning of time, God had planned for Thelma to realize this desire by serving those who lived in isolation. However, during her days in training, an incident occurred in Thelma's life that gave her vision a new relevance beyond mere adventurism.

During her growing up years, Thelma's spiritual life, while devout, was narrow and mechanical. The Bible, pulsating with life to one whose spirit is in tune and in obedient submission to God through His Son Jesus, was to her barren, uninteresting, and irrelevant to her everyday needs and experience. It wasn't that she was unaware of God being present in the world. She knew Him to be the Heavenly Father who created all things. Thus, Thelma knew *about* God, and on some occasions even went beyond her recited bedtime prayers to ask God for specific help. In fact, when she entered nurses' training, Thelma made a vow with God that if He helped her pass her studies, she would do anything for Him—even go to Africa!

Yet, because they had a rigid, somewhat legalistic approach to God, Thelma and her family hadn't fully understood that they, through Jesus Christ, could *know* God in a deep and personal way. Never in their lives had they experienced God in a relationship of childlike trust in Jesus Christ.

Then one day, shortly after she began her training, a group of "different" nurses invited Thelma to a small gathering of fellow nurses. The group turned out to be a chapter of the Nurses Christian Fellowship (NCF). Years later when Thelma recalled that event, she said, "It was that small group of Christian nurses who helped me understand that Jesus was more than an impersonal force. I learned that Jesus Christ wanted my friendship and love. Rather than being distant and impersonal, God showed me He wanted to be my intimate friend, a friend who I learned was more interested in me than I was in myself."

With a believing trust that came about through a decisive act of her will, Thelma chose the Son of Man as her Savior, Mentor, and Friend, and from that moment she purposed in her heart to learn all she could about this One who had died for her on a small hill called Calvary outside the city walls of Jerusalem so long ago.

Since she had come into the new relationship through the Nurses Christian Fellowship, it was only natural to continue as part of their weekly Bible study meeting. Later, when Thelma had a weekend off, she returned to her home in Galt. (She was studying in Brantford, twenty miles from her home town.) Immediately Thelma explained to her mother and brothers all that had happened. And when Thelma suggested they begin attending church, her mother and younger brother accepted her suggestion to attend nearby Forward Baptist Church. It was there, several Sundays later, that Thelma, in response to the pastor's invitation to come forward for baptism, walked the aisle. To her surprise, her younger brother fell in step beside her—not initially for baptism, but for salvation. Before that special Sunday when sister and brother were baptized, Thelma's mother indicated her desire to take Jesus as her personal Redeemer and Lord.

In an unexpected way, yet in keeping with her profession as a nurse, Thelma had brought healing and light to her family. It was the kind of light that went far beyond the stylized symbol of the Florence Nightingale lamp—a symbol that has come to mean care and healing within the nursing community. For Thelma, there was at once joy and sadness as she carried this "lamp" of spiritual light. Joy over her mother and younger brother's response, but sadness for her father and two older brothers who refused to be guided by this new light.

But Thelma had faith and believed the remainder of her family would come to understand how supremely Jesus loved them. In the meantime, she had the responsibility of giving serious attention to her studies.

And for a young woman who dreamed of nursing in a land of ice, snow, trappers, dog sleds, and Eskimos, getting there was most definitely *not* half the fun.

Without embarrassment, Thelma freely admitted she didn't like studying or going to school and that she was looking forward to her graduation ceremony as the end of ever having to study again. When one of her girlfriends from NCF suggested she one day attend Bible school to further her understanding of the Scriptures, Thelma responded with, "Bible school? Me go to Bible school? Listen, if I ever get through these years, I will have had it with school."

Thelma did get through those years, and in 1953, on May 8, she pinned on a stiffly starched white cap adorned with a velvet black band that would forever tell people she had graduated from the Brantford School of Nursing. However, rather than finding a nursing position in northern Canada, Thelma accepted one in her hometown of Galt. And rather than being overjoyed, it turned out to be one of the most difficult and profoundly lonely periods in her life.

Part of her loneliness came from post-graduation blues as she saw girlfriend after girlfriend get married or take exotic European or Caribbean vacations. In the face of being without friends and the hard reality of a daily routine that required a long walk from the hospital to her rented residence, Thelma's idealistic future quickly faded.

The only interruption to this routine was a weekly sponsorship of a NCF Chapter. But, in a reverse way, this sponsorship served only to intensify her loneliness. As a graduate Christian nurse, many of the student nurses believed Thelma was more mature and more knowledgeable in her faith than she actually felt she was. Even though Thelma was a growing Christian and had developed a regular devotional time of prayer and

Scripture reading, she felt woefully inadequate to lead or teach the student nurses in Bible study. And then one day in the midst of her extreme feelings of inadequacy, Thelma received a letter from an old friend who was attending London Bible College. "You really ought to come down to London and visit us," wrote Thelma's friend. Actually, this hadn't been the first time Thelma had received such a letter. Each time her friend had written she had urged Thelma to visit or consider attending the Bible school herself.

Up until she received this most recent letter, going to Bible school hardly seemed to make sense. But now it seemed to make perfect sense, and with the assurance that the Lord was leading her, Thelma wrote the London Bible School for an application and information.

While Thelma experienced a peace about her decision to change careers, her mother and father were troubled and perplexed. "What do you mean giving up your nurses' training for this . . . this notion of going to Bible school? Why do you want to do such a foolish thing? You are giving up something you've worked so hard to get and now you are throwing it all away. It just doesn't make sense. Why, it's hardly been a year since you graduated and here you go and quit your position to attend Bible school. I don't know when I've heard anything more ridiculous."

Thelma had expected some family opposition to her new idea, but never dreamed her mother would take it quite this hard. "Mother," said Thelma softly, "I simply can't go on forever doing what makes me feel miserable. Look at it this way—I spent three years learning about the body; now it's time I spent a little time learning about the soul."

Before the end of her first year at Bible school, Thelma was almost ready to concur with her mother that a shift in careers was indeed ridiculous. "I am overwhelmed by the sheer weight of new knowledge," she once said to a friend who asked about her progress. But by the end of the second year, Thelma's self-confidence had been strengthened by her good grades, and she settled in her mind that she was going in the right direction.

Part of what made her second year more enjoyable was gaining the new direction her life had taken. Her commitment to Jesus Christ and the desire to share this new experience of love with others coupled nicely with her own pioneering spirit. The result of this coupling produced the birth of an idea that grew into a desire to become a career missionary. Her only hesitation with this notion was having to learn a foreign language. "My worst subject in high school was French," she told a friend one day. "I barely passed it!"

Later, Thelma expressed to a teacher her intention of one day becoming a missionary and her fears about language learning. "There is a course being offered out west," said the teacher. "It's called the Summer Institute of Linguistics. I don't know what all that means, but I know many mission boards send their new workers for a summer of linguistic study before they go to their fields of service. In fact, I believe a few of our students have been thinking about taking the course this summer, especially since hearing that speaker in chapel from Wycliffe Bible Translators. One of them is Don Webster."

Thelma smiled. "Don Webster," she thought, "if only you knew how the girls in the dorm fight over you and how jealous they get when you date so many and hardly ask the same girl out twice."

Out of honest magnanimity, Don frequently dated a variety of college girls. Naively he assumed he could take out any girl just as one might ask out his sister. Little did he realize the pain, confusion, and jealousies he caused among the girls in the dorm.

Thelma hadn't paid too much attention to this outgoing young man the girls had nicknamed "Don Juan." But as she walked out of the classroom back to her own room, she wondered how the girls in the dorm would feel when they discovered she was going to spend the summer studying linguistics with the school's most available bachelor.

At 4:00 o'clock on a Friday afternoon, immediately after their last class, Don, a married couple who owned the car, Thelma, and her roommate Sinikka Suomela crammed themselves into the little vehicle and headed west across the prairies. For two nights and a day they did little more than drive, doze, snack, and drive some more. For more than 1800 miles the five people, mentally and physically exhausted from a hard winter and spring of studies, sped along the then partially completed Trans-Canada Highway. Their final destination was a nondescript dot on the map called Caronport, Saskatchewan.

In 1956, Caronport's claim to fame was the efficiently run Briercrest Bible School and private elementary and high school designed to educate the sons and daughters of evangelical prairie farmers. During World War II, Caronport had been a Royal Canadian Air Force training base. Wisely the trustees of the school acquired the leftover barracks, mess hall, gym, hangar, and tarmac that stretched out across the prairie grassland like a giant ribbon. It was here each summer that the Summer Institute of Linguistics (SIL), a sister organization to Wycliffe Bible Translators, Inc., held its linguistic courses.★ Except for a battered weather-worn train platform and grain silo, and a coffee shop that sported chrome tables and chairs, there was nothing but open prairies for as far as the eye could see. But for Don and

★This course has since moved to the University of Washington in Seattle.

Thelma, this was to become the most romantic spot on earth.

The romance began with an innocuous walk to the hangar the weekend after Don and Thelma arrived at SIL. A missionary family from Eskimo Point, west of Hudson Bay, had flown to Caronport in their own sleek Piper Four-Place aircraft. Don, who just a few months before had received his pilot's license, was all aglow with the wonders of the marvelous flying machine. In all the world there was nothing quite as exciting for Don as to hear the roar of the plane's engines and feel the force of power shudder beneath him as he sped down a tarmac and lifted off, upward into a clear golden sky. And what could be more perfect than having a pretty blue-eyed coed at your side who seemed to drink in every word you said.

And so the time was set—after the Friday night party when the fifty or so would-be translators and staff got together to unwind after a week of trying to figure out what linguistics was all about. With extra special care, Thelma saw to it that her soft brown curls were in perfect order.

Don greeted Thelma with his customary smile, a smile that is consistently warm and open, and together they stepped outside—into a drizzle. The rain wasn't the least bothersome to Don. He made the usual pedestrian remark about it being helpful for the farmers. But for Thelma, or more correctly her curls, the rain was a disaster.

For the next couple of hours Don explained how he had been attracted to missions after learning how Mission Aviation Fellowship (MAF) and Wycliffe's Jungle Aviation and Radio Service (JAARS) used planes in their mission outreach. After all, he explained, he had spent five years in the Air Force and felt the most practical and efficient use of his talent would be to work

with airplanes. And when with great interest Don examined the Piper in the hangar and enthusiastically told
Thelma how it all worked, Thelma smiled weakly, nodded, and said the "ah's" and "oh's" in what she hoped
were the right places. Then when there didn't seem too
much more to talk about, Don walked Thelma back to
the dorm, through the rain.

Convinced she had looked "simply awful" and
that Don would never ask her out again, Thelma shook
his hand, turned, and walked sadly back to her room.
But as it often is with men, Don's receptors were all
inward. All he had seen was the wonder of the flying
machine. And Thelma? Well, she was cute, whether her
hair was finely coiffured or wind- and rain-swept.

After a second week of linguistic study where the
students were being introduced to the different sounds
non-English speakers use to communicate and how to
imitate them, the students were more than ready for
their weekly Friday fun night. And again, Don asked
Thelma to go for a walk on the tarmac.

There was no rain this night. Just a clear, blue-
black sky studded with dancing stars that seemed close
enough for one to reach up and pluck right out of the
sky. There was a moon, of course. How could there not
be? And it was bright—bright enough to read by.

Don and Thelma were not the only couple to mix
romance with their studies. Others had seen the big,
bright moon and they, too, took to walking around the
tarmac. Conveniently, they were well spaced and often
walked in opposite directions. Thus began a weekly
ritual for Don and Thelma. On Friday nights they
walked to the hangar; on Saturday nights they walked
down the gravel Trans-Canada Highway. And it was
on this walk along the highway a week or two later that
Don and Thelma, in the manner of a Hollywood-
directed boy-meets-girl film, literally fell into each
other's arms. On their way back to the campus, Don

made an incorrect right-hand turn at the exact moment Thelma made the correct left-hand turn off the highway onto the path that led back to the school. Nothing could have been more perfect, and Don made the most of this unexpected opportunity. When they bumped into each other, Thelma gave a quick nervous laugh, but before she could say a word, Don wrapped his arms around her slender frame, leaned over, and kissed her tenderly.

About the fourth or fifth week into the SIL course, Don and Thelma were becoming aware that God was leading them in a way different from what both had perceived to be their reasons for coming to SIL. Don, with his interest and ability with aircraft, thought there would be a place for him in some sort of mission aviation program. But now, staring him in the face, was a new option—linguistics. Never in his wildest dreams did he believe he would become "hooked" on the study of grammar, or syntax and semantics, as they called it at SIL. Always before he thought the study of grammar, or anything to do with language, was pedantic, boring, and irrelevant to his everyday life. But here at SIL, Don came to understand in a new and exciting way how the study of linguistics had more to do with people, their cultures, and the psychology of language than it had to do with strict rules of grammar as taught in English classes. Here were at once some highly sophisticated, yet practical tools that would enable him to discover the working principles of an unwritten language. At the same time, linguistics seemed to satisfy his scientific, ideological, and spiritual aspirations. "It intrigued me," said Don, "that Wycliffe's method of giving people the Word of God in their own mother tongue was a functional way to do God's work. I began to feel that perhaps God was leading me into linguistics and Bible translation."

Don, of course, wasn't the only student that summer who was struggling with new options. Thelma was also going through her own metamorphosis. To her surprise, she discovered she had an aptitude for linguistics. The interaction between the various methods of inquiry a linguist would use to explore and explain the mysteries and complexities of an unwritten language were, to her, like working a great interlocking puzzle. And yet while she felt she could pursue a career as a Bible translator, she deferred to her roommate Sinikka.

Sinikka shone that summer as a brilliant linguist. Believing they would be partners together with Wycliffe on a particular field, Thelma said she would be the nurse and Sinikka the Bible translator. That was, of course, before Don Webster came into the picture. Yet, while she enjoyed Don and they had in a casual way been going steady all summer, Don hadn't made his intentions known. Thelma didn't even know if he planned to join Wycliffe. It wasn't until after the Day of Prayer that Thelma understood a true metamorphosis was about to take place in her life.

5

The Meeting

Roy Ahmaogak first met Turner Blount, then director of Wycliffe's work in North America, in 1956 at a meeting of Presbyterian pastors and elders in Fairbanks, Alaska. Turner had more than a passing interest in providing the Scriptures for ethnic minority peoples of North America. He had been part of a translation team that provided the New Testament for the Navajo people of Arizona. Of particular interest to him were two more groups without the Scriptures in their own language. One was the Inupiat Eskimos living in Alaska's North Slope; the other, while not strictly falling under his supervision, was the peoples of Siberia.

Implicit in Turner's duties as director was the evaluation of the need of a translation for those ethnic minorities (often called the hidden people of the world) and the allocation of translation teams to those areas. On one of his evaluation trips, Turner made a special effort to meet Roy and learn about his translation program. It was common knowledge among those in the translation community that Roy was eager for the Scriptures in his own mother tongue.

The meeting between the two men was a happy mixture of friendly laughter over experiences both had shared at SIL, and there was much talk about the need of an Inupiat translation. Part of that meeting revealed Roy's need for more translation time. "If only there was someone from your organization who could help me in the general duties of the pastorate. If such a person could come to live with us in Wainwright Village where I have my church, then I could spend more time on translation."

Turner didn't forget Roy's pleas for help and about a year later wrote him the following letter with a copy going to Don and Thelma.

Dec. 2, 1957

Dear Roy,

I have thought often about our happy time of fellowship in Fairbanks. You will remember the principal subject of conversation centered around the need for Scripture translation for the people of your area. We also talked about your heavy schedule and the need for someone to help you get on with the job of translation.

As you know, Wycliffe is an organization dedicated to Bible translation. We have found that unless someone makes translation their principal occupation, the translation won't get done, even as you yourself have admitted. We have two people, recently married, who we feel would be ideal helpers in your translation project. Their names are Don and Thelma Webster.

The Websters couldn't spend too much time in general mission work, but Don has shown great linguistic talent and we feel, as he does, too, that God is calling him to Bible translation and associated projects such as literacy and linguistic research.

Their first assignment would be to learn the language. This is no small task. Many non-Inupiat speakers have tried and failed. However, we believe the training the Websters received at SIL will greatly help them in this area.

In January, the Websters will be going to Wycliffe's

Jungle Camp in southern Mexico for further training. In addition to this, we have asked that Don take a summer session studying with the Canadian Linguistic Society at the University of Alberta in Edmonton.

Turner's letter continued with some further remarks about how he hoped the Websters could help Roy in practical ways, such as typing, perhaps holding reading classes, and in language analysis. There was a sentence about how wonderful it was that Roy under God's leading had become so burdened for the spiritual development of his own people. Turner ended the letter by telling Roy he would have the Websters write directly to him about any questions they might have. And that was that. Except Turner added a postscript Roy never saw. In a single paragraph, Turner outlined for Don and Thelma a delicate problem they would face.

It is quite a shock to Roy to actually be faced with someone else coming in on his job of translation. Roy is most competent, but I don't think he would ever finish the job even if he had all the time in the world. It is just too big a job, and too confining. Roy is a spiritual man and wants the will of the Lord in this task. We will go slow and drop the seeds of conditioning along the way. I think he will come around and let you do whatever needs to be done. It's good (psychologically) that there is some time for preparation. From your standpoint, I am sure it doesn't matter who gets credit for a translation, just as long as it gets done and people read it. Glad you like marriage. God intended it that way. Drop me a carbon of your letter to Roy.

Turner was right. God's design is for men and women to become one in marriage and to experience joyous love and companionship. It is in this way that the fusion of two into one makes both persons stronger than either of them could be alone. And in every way Don and Thelma were experiencing this new euphoria along with the unexpected burrs and adjustments that come when two individuals agree to live together in such a dynamic relationship.

For the best of reasons, Don and Thelma had agreed to marry. Both wanted personal intimacy and companionship. Linked with this was a spiritual oneness—a unifying and transcendent power outside themselves—the Lordship of Jesus Christ. Further, they both had been called independently to a work of noble purpose.

For Don, the countdown for marriage to Thelma began at the end of the Day of Prayer at Caronport.

Toward the end of the linguistics course, the SIL staff planned a day free of classroom study for those considering applying to Wycliffe to give themselves to prayer. For many this step of faith—aligning themselves with Wycliffe as a career missionary—would be one of the most important and crucial decisions of their lives. The SIL staff wanted each one to be fully persuaded in his or her own minds and hearts that this decision was prompted by what they perceived to be God's will for them.

For Thelma, the decision to join Wycliffe was clear-cut. There was never a doubt that God was leading her, and before the end of the day, she submitted her application. For Don, the decision wasn't as well defined. He battled a shadow of uncertainty of whether to join Wycliffe or not. About the only thing he felt certain about was that linguistics had edged out flying as a career. And then as he perused the Scriptures for some word of encouragement, of insight and guidance, his eyes stopped at verses 23 and 24 of Psalm 73: "Nevertheless I am continually with you; You hold me by my right hand. Thou shalt guide me with Thy counsel, and afterward receive me to glory."

As he read and reread these verses, Don was impressed with the detail inherent in the phrase, "You (God) hold me by my right hand." Don knew the Psalmist was using figurative language, but it was all Don needed. "If God is holding me by my right hand," he reasoned, "it means He is doing so with His left hand, thus leaving His right hand free for battle and victory."

Later that evening, Don, like Thelma, submitted his application to serve the Lord through Wycliffe as a Bible translator wherever they felt his talent would serve them best. These few verses had given him the confidence to believe that no matter what problem, difficulty, or heartache he might encounter in this new adventure, God would always be beside him, holding and supporting him in the battle.

The next day at noon, after the grueling morning classes, Don learned the truth of the promise that the one who seeks first the Kingdom of God shall have other things added to him. In Don and Thelma's case it was each other. As they talked over the events of the preceding day, they learned each had applied without the knowledge of the other. At that moment, the marriage light blinked on in Don's mind. That fall, Don and Thelma returned to the London Bible Institute where their relationship deepened, and that Christmas Don slipped a ring onto Thelma's finger.

A strength and weakness of Don's personality is his need to see measurable and attainable goals. During his second summer at SIL after graduating from London Bible Seminary, this time at Norman, Oklahoma,*

---

*Currently, SILs are conducted in four university locations in the U.S. In 1958, Norman, Oklahoma was the usual place to send second-year students for their advanced linguistic studies.

Don ran into a linguistic jungle with no visible way out. Part of the problem was an incomplete linguistic formula that produced incorrect conclusions.

For a time, this inability to handle and make sense out of his linguistic data caused Don to rethink the direction he was taking. When he discussed this with Thelma and suggested perhaps he would be better suited to being a chaplain in the air force, Thelma's heart sank. Almost from the begining of her linguistic studies at Caronport, she had been convinced God had led her into Wycliffe. For a few anxious days it seemed all they had prayed and talked about in Caronport, and in her final year at London Bible Institute was about to be scuttled. But by the end of the summer, the linguistic problem was solved and Don was back on track again.

A few short weeks after their second summer at SIL, Don and Thelma were married. The date was September 14, 1957, and after that splendid moment, events in the Websters' life moved rapidly. In October, to reacquaint himself and his new bride with the members and friends of his home church, Don and Thelma set up housekeeping in Montreal. There Don became the assistant pastor at Peoples Church, the same church where many years before he had come under conviction and walked the aisle in open testimony of his desire to follow the Lord as his personal Savior.

While Don performed his pastoral duties, Thelma did what she was trained to do—nurse. The mother of a longtime friend of Don's had recently become an invalid through a massive stroke, and Thelma lovingly cared for her. Three months later in January 1958, after visiting and enjoying Christmas with both sets of parents, Don and Thelma were on their way to take further training at Wycliffe's Jungle Camp in southern Mexico.

In the meantime, Turner Blount had been in conversation with Don and Thelma about working in Alaska. And the more Turner explained the interesting and somewhat unique situation with Roy and the Inupiat, the more Don and Thelma became convinced this was where God would have them serve.

And so after Bible school, after two summers at SIL, after a marriage, after Jungle Camp in southern Mexico, after a special summer of linguistic study in Edmonton, and after enduring a bundle of joys, disappointments, and frustrations, Don and Thelma finally arrived in Nenana, Alaska. It was September 1, 1958. As director of Wycliffe's North America Branch, Turner Blount knew the Arctic was most unforgiving toward those who trespassed her terrain without knowing the rules for survival. And when Don and Thelma arrived in Nenana, it was in time to begin, with several other new workers, a training exercise called Arctic Camp. Actually the camp wasn't due to begin until sometime in October. Don couldn't have been happier. This interim gave him just enough time to fly out to Wainwright Village, find a house, and meet the legendary Roy Ahmaogak. Don quickly wrote advising him that he would be coming as soon as he could get Thelma settled.

Since that first meeting with Roy in 1956, Turner had been quietly orchestrating an eventual meeting between Don and Roy. At Turner's suggestion, Don had first contacted Roy while he was at Jungle Camp. In his letter he expressed his interest and desire to work with Roy and be part of the translation team for the Inupiat New Testament. Roy had responded with a typewritten letter on the official stationery of the Ulgunik Presbyterian Church in Wainwright, Alaska. Walter Nayakik was listed as the Clerk of Session, David Panik as the organist, and Roy Ahmaogak as the Missionary Pastor.

Dear Brother in Christ:

I was happy to receive your letter. Isn't it wonderful to know each other in the Lord even without having met in person? Indeed, it is wonderful to know that the Kingdom of our Lord goes beyond the boundary of creed and color. It always thrills my heart to realize that somewhere someone is thinking of us and praying on our behalf in the service we strive to do for our common Lord and Savior.

I have thanked Him again and again for the opportunity He gave me to have a year of study in the States, three months in the linguistic school of the Wycliffe Bible Translators in Norman, Oklahoma, and the rest of the year at Bloomfield Seminary in New Jersey. That study has helped me a lot in my present work here under the Board of National Missions of the Presbyterian Church, USA. But I am sorry that my translation work has been slowed and somewhat crowded out of my work as Missionary Pastor.

May I tell you that I sincerely appreciate your offer of assistance with the translation of the Bible into our Eskimo language. It isn't so much help in the translation work itself that I need, but in the total program of the Church here, some of which could be relieved and carried on by an assistant. This would no doubt give me time for my translation work.

I have discussed this problem of time for translation work with my Sunday School teachers and church officers, but so far we have come to no decision. My conviction is that the translation of the Bible is a must, but we are failing, at least for the time being. Many illiterates have found joy and comfort in learning to read my translation of the Gospel of Mark and Epistle to the Romans. I can never forget the remark made by a young woman when she learned to read the translation. She said, "Though I could see the Bible with my eyes, I was like a blind person, because when I opened it I could not read a word of English. When the translation came out, I was like a blind person receiving her sight, because I learned to read the Word of God in my own tongue."

Well, so much for that, and now to answer your question, is there a house available at Wainwright? . . .

From this point on, Roy's letter was less precise, especially about housing. Yes, he thought there might be an apartment in the schoolhouse that "may or may not be rented." As to furniture, Roy suggested the Websters buy whatever they need "in the lower forty-eight and have it shipped. Shipping is always cheaper than buying in Alaska."

In his letter, Don had also asked about fuel for their house. Roy wrote about a nearby coal mine where everyone went to mine their own, free of charge. He did add that the government school had oil shipped in and added he wished they could do the same. As to Don's question about how cold it became in Wainwright, Roy answered matter-of-factly that it was always "several degrees below zero, with heavy blasts of wind and snow and without trees to break the force of the wind when the storms come." Roy then ended his letter with the following paragraph:

> It was good to note in your letter that you and your wife have both given your lives completely to the Lord for His service anywhere in the world and it is your belief that you should begin by coming to our area. It is my prayer that the Lord will bless you and direct you in the work where He needs you most. I am sure He has a place for you where you can render service for Him and to His glory. God bless you.
>
> Sincerely in his service,
> Roy Ahmaogak (signed)

Don's flight from Fairbanks to Wainwright Village took him first over the spectacular Brooks Range and then 330 miles north of the Arctic Circle to the village of Barrow. In 1958, the community of Barrow had little more than 1000 Inupiat, but it was then and is today the largest Inupiat community in Alaska.

From Barrow, Don transferred to a Cessna 180

and flew ninety miles west along the coast to Wainwright. If the weather held, total flying time from Fairbanks to Wainwright with a stopover in Barrow was a little over five hours. And on this occasion, Don arrived on the heels of a storm that had just blown itself out.

As the pilot leaned forward on his wheel to begin his descent, he pointed out across a sea of white. "Wainwright coming up," he said. In the clear western light, Don could see a long thin coastline where from the beginning of time, wind and sea currents, ice and snow, had washed and ground the beach gravel into multiple layers of gleaming black ridges. As they banked for the final approach, Don noticed there was an indentation in the coastline that formed an island lagoon shaped like a stomach. Off to one side were thirty-five to forty nondescript wooden houses scattered over the tundra as carelessly as a child might scatter his building blocks.

"Where's the landing strip?" asked Don.

"We land where we can," said the pilot with a reassuring smile. "The people put out markers on the safe spots."

When the plane finally touched down on the uneven snow-covered tundra, Don expected Roy to be there to welcome him. He wasn't.

"I sent a letter more than a week ago," said Don.

"With all this bad weather we've been having, your letter might still be in Fairbanks. Or it could be here in this mail pouch. In any case, even though they will be surprised to see you, they are always happy to have visitors. The manse is an easy mile from here."

In a couple of minutes a racing sled came slapping over the rough tundra. It was Peter Tagarook, the mailman, coming to collect the mail pouch. After a happy exchange with the pilot, Peter told Don to hold on tight and off they sped toward the village. As the spirited team bounded over the tundra, intensifying the sharpness of the arctic wind, a strange surge of joy began to race through Don's body. Here he was in the place where for so many years God had been directing him, and now at long last it was actually happening. For a moment as they bounced along, a kind of overpowering fullness stuck in his chest and he wanted to shout for joy.

The pilot was right—in no time they were in the village and Peter pointed out the manse. As Don approached, he noticed two men trying to break in a team of young dogs, put them in their traces, and hitch them up to a sled. The two men were Roy and his son Benny. For one who had almost no experience with sled dogs, this display of eight assorted canines barking, lunging, thumping, bumping, leaping this way and that, and Roy jumping into the middle of the mad scramble to keep them in order while he harnessed the lead dog, was worth the expensive flight to Wainwright.

Discreetly Don waited until what seemed to him an impossible task was completed, and then introduced himself. And again the pilot was right. Roy hadn't received Don's letter and was most surprised to find this young man suddenly drop out of the sky. And as predicted, Roy was, as all the villagers, most friendly and welcomed him warmly.

After the preliminary introductions were over, Roy affirmed Don's coming by suggesting perhaps the Lord had indeed sent him at just this particular time.

"Do you preach?" asked Roy blandly.

"Yes, I do," said Don, "and I enjoy it when I have the opportunity."

"Good," said Roy, "because beginning tonight we start our yearly preaching mission. And as it sometimes happens, I overlooked arranging for a special speaker. Yes, I believe the Lord has sent you here to be our speaker."

For the next five days, Wainwright's 250 people learned firsthand how the Lord had dealt with and led Don's steps to their village. They also learned that in many ways Don was a no-nonsense kind of man who believed strongly in a spiritually disciplined life. Sprinkled throughout his messages were concepts about being faithful to the responsibilities God had given each person to perform. In all, the truths were important and orthodox. But later one man commented that Don's messages were almost too strong; that there was a critical edge to his sermons. "Perhaps a message that reflected a softening of one's heart would have been more appropriate."

Don received this criticism as a compliment. It affirmed to himself he was saying exactly what the people needed to hear. As far as softening of one's heart, well, he didn't know about that. He felt people needed to be told the truth in a "thus saith the Lord" fashion.

But Don was young, and he was winsome and most open and friendly, and even with his strong words, he won their hearts as they won his. In fact, Don was so content at Roy's house with its warmth of personality and household smells of stew or soup simmering on the stove, that he jokingly said he wished a blizzard would come and keep him snowbound for the winter.

It wasn't to be, of course. He still had to return to Nenana and go through Arctic Training Camp. As Don thought about returning, he admitted to Roy that he was getting a little tired of training programs. "All I want to do is go back and get Thelma and settle down to learn the Inupiat language and find a house where we can live."

"Ah, yes, the house," said Roy. "I think I have one for you."

Roy then told Don about a house owned by a rather tight-fisted trader, who, in Roy's words, "hadn't yet turned his life over to the Lord. You may be able to rent it inexpensively as it's small, and he hasn't lived in it for at least ten years."

Roy's comment about the house being small was a gross understatement. It was a twelve by fifteen foot cabin with a sleeping loft under the hip roof. The windows were boarded up. When the two men opened the door, Don could tell that indeed it hadn't been lived in for ten years.

The men entered the house by opening a door to an antechamber or shed. This faced out to sea, away from the prevailing winds. They then passed through yet another shed-type room and opened the door to the main room. To enter, they stepped over a small ledge and down onto the floor that was several inches below ground level. As Don surveyed the interior of this little house that was to be his and Thelma's home for the next ten years, his stomach gave a quick jolt.

Without embarrassment, Don freely admits he isn't the most aesthetically sensitive person in the world, but the color scheme in this room gave him great difficulty. From floor to waist-height the room was painted battleship gray, with a lighter gray above that. It was the most hideous, dark, dingy room Don had ever seen.

Don knew Thelma would have greater difficulty with the colors than he, but there was no alternative. There was no time to build, and even if there had been, building supplies were expensive and would take a year to get there. Roy wanted the Websters to come, and while the rent at $40.00 per month was high, it was affordable. Feeling he had accomplished his mission, Don returned to Nenana and resumed the last requirement of his training—Arctic Camp.

In 1958, there were eight new families plus several single women who took part in this winter exercise. For Don, who had grown up in Ontario with snow and ice, much of what was being taught seemed redundant. But Don, being Don, went along with only a minimum of resistance.

Following the American Air Force Manual for Arctic Survival, the translators were equipped physically and mentally with tools and techniques that would enable them to survive situations found nowhere else on earth. They learned little things like how to fish through the ice. The trick is to not make the hole too big and keep it ice-free long enough to get your fish out.

Women as well as men learned how to handle and shoot rifles heavy enough to bring down a grizzly, caribou, or moose. They also learned how to dress, cook, and eat the game they shot.

They were made aware of little, but decisively important, tricks like not becoming too hot when running a dog team. The danger of perspiring in twenty to thirty degrees below is the danger of freezing to death from the inside out when you begin to cool down.

Along with the myriad of practical skills were the watchwords that came to be second nature to them. Words like, "The Arctic is made for winter. Think ahead! Beware of freeze up and break up in the spring. Planes can't land on their skis or floats or wheels in slush or mud. Think ahead! Even dogsleds can't cross rivers or be out on the ice in the spring thaw when the water drains away and exposes the candle ice that is as sharp and dangerous as splintered glass. Think ahead, particularly if you're going to have a baby."

These were wise words and particularly applicable to Don and Thelma since their first child was due in April.

6

Patience-Triers

For two months the sun had hidden itself below the horizon. The only hint that it hadn't completely died was a slight lightening on the southern skyline each day at noon if the sky wasn't overcast. Ever since late November the people in Wainwright had guided themselves only by the cold clear light of the winter moon. But on this day, January 14, 1959, under a clear sky, the twilight seemed to stretch extra long into the day. It brought a surge of anticipation to the villagers who eagerly counted the days of another week before the timid sun would reappear on the rim of their world.

Something else rippled excitement through that day. The local gossip was that Don Webster and his young wife, Thelma, were coming to set up housekeeping in the trader's old house, this against the advice of Pastor Ahmaogak who had warned them not to move in the dead of winter. "Wait until spring," he had said in a letter. But the Websters felt the Lord didn't enjoy delays any more than they did and decided to come in spite of Roy's contrary warning.

Back in November, on the exact day the sun decided to hibernate, Don's supervisor in Alaska asked if they could get ready to move to Wainwright by January 15, no later.

"How much time do we have to decide?" asked Don.

"About half an hour," said the supervisor.

Immediately Don and Thelma began to calculate how much money they had★ and asked the Lord to guide them in this unexpected but exciting new prospect. They, with other new workers, had completed about six weeks of Arctic Camp training, and the plan was to stay at Nenana until after Christmas and move to the village in the spring. But the influx of new Wycliffe workers had put a strain on the limited huts rented for the occasion. In reality, the center needed Webster's little skid bunkhouse they called home ever since they had arrived in September. But the Websters didn't mind being asked to leave. The problem forced them to make a decision, and they decided to move to Wainwright by January 14. Now came the logistics of working out exactly how to arrange for the transportation of their food and equipment.

One of the most critical pieces of equipment was a stove, a stove they hadn't yet purchased. There was also the matter of housing. After inspecting the little house in Wainwright, Don had contacted the trader, but as yet hadn't received his final permission to rent it. It seemed the trader wanted $45.00 instead of $40.00 per month. Don knew he couldn't wait until he heard from the

---

★All Wycliffe members must, in faith, depend upon God to supply their temporal needs. Wycliffe as an organization provides no guaranteed allowance or income for its members. Wycliffe does, however, carefully forward all money designated by donors to specific members.

trader and then order the stove from Seattle. There wouldn't be time to have it shipped and set up to pre-heat the house before they arrived. Therefore, believing the man of faith is an audacious man, Don ordered the stove from Sears in Seattle and asked that it be shipped as soon as possible.

Next came the gigantic problem of ordering food. Most women do their weekly shopping from a hastily scribbled shopping list. And if an item should be missed, no matter. It can easily be picked up the next day at the local supermarket. Thelma had no such option. The only way supplies could reach them economically was to have a year's supply shipped in on the North Star. This 5000-ton liberty-type freighter serviced government schools, the hospital, and cooperative stores along the 2000-mile Alaska coast from the Aleutians to Barrow. Before the Websters could ship their items, however, they had to get permission from the Commison Company, a mail order house in Seattle that handled all shipments on the North Star. But before they could get permission, they had to know the cubic capacity and weight of their whole shipment that would include items other than food. Additionally, if permission was granted, the Websters were required to prepay half the cost of their order. "It was," wrote Don matter-of-factly, "a large task and a large bill."

In the meantime, Don and Thelma ordered some food items they would need immediately from a wholesaler in Anchorage. Since weight was of the essence, at that time about twenty-one cents per pound for air freight, they decided to buy everything dried. And since dried red kidney beans had been a staple in Jungle Camp, they decided this should be their main staple. They also bought dried peas and potatoes, and rice. Next came dried peaches and apples along with soup powders and tea. At first Don had planned to air freight everything into Wainwright, but after checking around, he providentially discovered he could use the postal services and mail in his supplies for ten cents per pound.

Little by little things began to fall into place. The Websters did receive clearance to ship on the North Star and some unexpected money that came in at Christmas enabled them to prepay and ship all their goods. In his diary Don wrote:

> After a discouraging struggle with low finances and wondering how we would pay for all our food and equipment, God has done abundantly above all that we could ask or think. All glory be to His Name.

All that remained now was to coordinate their transportation schedules and notify Roy they would arrive January 14. Don wanted to be sure their arrival in Wainwright wouldn't be like his first visit, when no one was there to meet him. And it wasn't.

As before, the plane landed by the guidance of markers set out by the people. Instead of landing on uneven tundra as it had previously, the Cessna 180 landed on the iced-over lagoon, the one shaped like a big stomach. Since this was the mail plane, the man who came for the mail also collected Don and Thelma and drove them back to the center of Wainwright in his dog sled.

In 1959 the heart of this Inupiat village of 250 people was the post office. And like the village, it was small. Very small. Thelma described it as being about the size of an oversized packing crate. But small or not, it was warm, both from a heater and from the people standing around waiting for their mail, who greeted them with open smiles and handshakes.

At first Thelma didn't quite know what to make of what she thought was a strange way to begin shaking one's hand. Garbed in traditional ankle-length fur parkas with loose fitting sleeves, the women, as was their custom when standing and visiting, had slipped their arms out of their sleeves and folded them across their chest, placing their hands under their armpits for warmth. Therefore, to perform the courtesy of hand-shaking, the women quickly jerked their right hand back into their sleeve with a vigorous swirling motion until their hands poked through the fur-trimmed cuff to grasp Thelma's uneasy hand.

With their greetings over, and with the happy expectancy of two and a half more people being added to the village (the Inupiat women nodded their happy approval over Thelma's noble pregnant state), Roy and several others led the way to the Webster cabin.

Thelma had no idea what to expect. Don had been characteristically vague about the details that most interest a woman. And when she saw the Cessna 180 take off shortly after they landed, it suddenly came to her that she was, for the next five years, absolutely land-locked. "I'm stuck," she thought. "There are no roads, no cars, and how far can you go in a dog sled?" Admittedly they were fragmentary thoughts amid all the confusion of being welcomed and trying to concentrate on all that was happening.

And part of what was happening gave her, like it had given Don earlier, a deep sense of awe. She was finally here in the God-appointed place for which she had trained. But the other half of her emotions were not quite as idealistic. She had been overwhelmed by the blanket of white snow covering Wainwright for as far as the eye could see. The post office, while small, was cute and the people friendly. So far she felt she could handle most anything. But then she walked into the house Don had selected for their home among the Inupiat.

After passing through the outer sheds that serve to

trap cold air from entering the main living quarters, Thelma stepped down into the main room of dismal gray. There she stopped. Even before she turned to look at him, Don could feel what was about to happen. Thelma said not a word. They were unnecessary. She simply turned and with a classic look known only to husbands and misbehaving children, said with her clear blue eyes, "I've got to live here?"

Thelma felt she could handle the depressing gray paint and the plain board floor that was beginning to be more visible as a young girl vigorously swept up ten years of dust and debris. Even the boarded-up windows didn't bother her, nor the lack of furniture. What prompted the look from those plaintive blue eyes was the walls. They were covered with thick hoarfrost. And so intense was the cold that the nails in many of the boards had popped out and were themselves covered with frost. Don had assured his young wife that the stove they had ordered would be set up and glowing hot to warm the house before their arrival.

But no such thing occurred. Roy informed Don the stove had arrived only two days before. "I suppose the shippers in Barrow overlooked it, or they didn't think it was too important to get down here since you hadn't arrived," said Roy. Thelma looked at her new, black, stone-cold stove. An old Inupiat woman was trying unsuccessfully to light a fire in it with some equally black coal and old pieces of cardboard. Inwardly she wanted to cry, but she didn't. She did what thousands of pioneer wives have done before her. She immediately set to work to make her nest livable for herself and her husband.

Don quickly unpacked their Coleman gas stove and set some water on for tea. Thelma, with Don's help, unboarded the windows and made up the three-quarter-size bed Roy had brought over for them to use.

Next a card table and some chairs appeared, and from their closest neighbors came a large chunk of caribou meat and several dozen smelt.

It soon became clear that the stove Don had purchased was woefully inadequate to stave off the penetrating cold. Without a word of ridicule or reproach, Homer Bodfish, a descendant of a famous nineteenth-century Yankee whaling captain, graciously loaned Don and Thelma an oil heater complete with a tank of oil. "This is for the upstairs sleeping loft," he said. "The house will never become warm with just one stove."

By January 19, five days after their arrival, Don noted in his journal that the little house was beginning to look a little more like home. The one frustration was the cold that in the mornings seemed almost unbearable. No matter how hard he stoked up the fire, the cold dissipated the heat almost before he had closed the cast-iron door. Thus trying to keep warm occupied most of his time. On January 17 he wrote: "Fire and coal are great patience-triers. My defeats are greater numerically than my victories."

The house never did become fully warm that entire winter. Don noted in his diary that after ten days, with both stoves going, there was still frost hanging on the back walls. In fact, the frost never did melt until June when it became "a little warmer."

The real problem of inadequate heat was not so much the stove but the coal. Don had grown up using the hot burning, almost smokeless anthracite, or hard coal. And this coal was lignite, or soft coal, that had washed up on the beaches or was mined a short distance away in an abandoned shaft and had about half the heating capacity and endurance of the hard coal. Don realized he had never asked what *kind* of coal was available when Roy had written him that there was coal available for fuel.

But cold and coal were only part of Don's preoccupation. His other concern was Roy. When Turner Blount had visited Don in Fairbanks, he indicated that Roy might lose interest in the translation when it came to the nitty-gritty, day-to-day routine of desk work. "Roy will be enthusiastic at first," Turner had said, "and your job will be to keep that enthusiasm high."

Turner never knew how prophetic his words would be. Within the first week, Roy visited Don and Thelma and asked casually, "When are we going to start translating?" For Roy it was the most natural of questions. After all, he knew his own language with all its beautiful subtleties and for years had read from his English Bible and interpreted from English into his native Inupiatun language. On the surface, this method of what Roy called translation seemed to work.

For Don, however, this was not what true translation was all about. In later years Don was to admit that at this time Roy knew infinitely more about translating than he. What Don did know was that translation was one of the most demanding and difficult of the literary arts. The weight and greatness of Scripture and its unique relation to God and His message to mankind demanded a most careful understanding of both the original languages and, in this case, the Inupiatun language. And Don hardly knew more than a simple greeting in Inupiatun.

Don's ability with original Greek was then also limited. He had to rely, as most translators do, on commentaries and a variety of English versions of the Bible, and as yet none of his books had arrived. Thus with Turner's words ringing in his ears, "Keep Roy's interest in the translation high," Don suggested to Roy they wait until the books arrived and he had learned some of the language.

This unexpected request from Roy to begin translation immediately presented Don with a unique problem. His assignment from Turner was to learn the language and check out the Inupiatun orthography to see if it followed as closely as possible the standard English alphabet.* He was also to test the language for clarity of grammatical construction. This would be necessary to see if indeed the Inupiatun Scriptures communicated in a natural, easy style. Roy would be discouraged to learn his work with Rev. Fred Klerekoper might not be acceptable to the Bible Society, and so all this investigation had to be done without his knowledge.

There was also the unique manner in which Roy translated. While it was immediately evident to Don that Roy surpassed him in translation ability, he knew to translate from English to Inupiatun was incorrect. Yet he did not want to discourage Roy, and so after a month of studying Inupiatun for at least eight to ten hours daily, and believing he could no longer make excuses for not getting down to the business of translation, Don set up a translation schedule of three evenings per week.

Initially, Don was pleased to be actually working, as he wrote, "so soon on translation." Most translators don't attempt to translate for at least twelve to eighteen months. Thelma, too, was pleased and did her part to pique Roy's interest in translation by baking bread, cookies, and biscuits. And she made sure Roy's tea was brewed to an inky blackness. He did enjoy his tea!

Roy was most appreciative of this attention, particularly his tea. But as the Websters were soon to discover, all this extra attention was unnecessary. Turner's

*One of the requirements of the American Bible Society, who would ultimately publish the Inupiatun New Testament, is that the orthography should conform as closely as possible to the national language of the country in which the ethnic minority resides, in this case English.

prediction of Roy as one who would quickly lose interest in the nitty-gritty of translation work was incorrect.

True to his natural bent to establish measurable goals, Don worked out a systematic plan to complete the translation of the New Testament in record time. Using his Revised Standard Bible with its double columns as a guide, Don showed Roy how they would complete the New Testament in three years and three months if they translated a column and a half per night. And this would allow time out to hunt. "I don't know if it was this measurable goal out in front that did it," said Don, "but when we came together to work on translation, Roy sat down and just as if someone had clicked on a switch, he would work like a machine. He never knew when to quit."

While Don and Thelma struggled to understand this new and most complicated language, they also struggled with the daily hazards of life in the Arctic. The first of these hazards occurred just a few days after Don and Roy began translating. One afternoon Don and Thelma were out visiting and returned to discover that the oil tank had sprung a leak. An oil slick (kerosene) had seeped its way all over the upstairs floor, down the stairs leading up to the loft, and through the ceiling onto the floor of the main room. To make matters worse, the upstairs walls, thick with frost and ice, were beginning to thaw and drip. It was, as Don wrote in his usual understatement, "an awful mess and a miserable job to clean up."

The second incident involved Thelma more than Don, and while it involved no messy cleanup, it did cause Thelma to reestablish her priorities. One of the first couples to befriend the Websters were Ruth and Wilson Eckles, school teachers for the village of Wainwright. They with their two sons, ages eleven and thirteen, made it a practice to meet once a week after Don's long hard week of study to roast popcorn and play parlor games, especially a hockey game. So intense were these games that the boys practiced all week long in hopes of beating the former high school ice hockey goalie. But they never did. Don's reflexes with the game's metal arms were just as fast as they had been with the real wooden stick. These were important moments of relaxation for Don and Thelma, and often they ended their fun evening with a prayer meeting.

When the Eckles learned that Thelma was a nurse and better than seven months pregnant, they feared for her health and suggested she not tell anyone that she had such skills. "If you do," said Ruth Eckles, "you'll be called out at all hours of the night, and getting over the sleek snow drifts in your condition will certainly cause you problems."

At the time it seemed like good advice. But then a neighbor's three-month-old daughter became sick. At first Thelma was unaware of this illness until Wilson Eckles asked Thelma to look in on the child.

"I don't think she will live," said Wilson. "Since it's so close, perhaps you could look in on her. Her name is Rosey."

One look with her practiced eye told Thelma the child was in the last stages of pneumonia. Immediately Thelma set up a steam tent and asked Wilson to allow her to use the medicines in the local clinic. At that time the government clinic was set up in the schoolhouse. Thelma knew the medicines would probably be ineffective, but she had to try.

All night long Thelma watched over little Rosey until she herself could hardly keep awake. At 4:00 A.M., Thelma returned home to rest for a couple of hours. At 6:00, with the snow beneath her boots sounding like someone twisting Styrofoam packing and with the pale yellow beam of her flashlight picking out the uneven spots in the tundra, she returned. Her flashlight guided her through the inky darkness of three outer sheds until she came to the main entrance and knocked softly. Everyone except the father was asleep. With deep concern in her voice she asked after Rosey's condition. "She's there in the box," he said blandly, then stooped to take the lid off the little box. Rosey's stiffened form struck Thelma with a numbing jolt.

Throughout her professional nursing career, Thelma had seen many people die. Often she had ministered spiritually and professionally to surviving family members going through grief. Some wept uncontrollably; others held their grief in check; but nonetheless there was clear evidence of heartbreak. But not so with this father. Never before had she witnessed such stoicism in the loss of one so close.

She, like Don, had read anthropological accounts of female infanticide among some Eskimo groups and in the short time since their arrival in Wainwright were beginning to understand "survival suicide." The unwritten law for people living in this extremely hostile environment was survival of the whole. This meant only those who filled a needful role or could hunt and gather food had a right to live. Those in a non-food-procuring role—often the older people—voluntarily committed suicide, thus allowing food needed to sustain them to go to a hunter.

The method of committing such a suicide was simply exposure to the elements. This could be done by hopping on an ice floe or losing oneself in a blizzard or walking out onto the tundra. Others committed suicide by slipping a rawhide noose over their necks with one end tied securely to an immovable object. They would then slump forward, strangling themselves. But none of this had been practiced in Wainwright for many years.

This was a truly Christian village. The Inupiat people clearly evidenced love and care for their children and older people as well.

In the face of the evidence before her, Thelma could only conclude that these lovely, warm-hearted people had come to expect and accept a fifty-fifty mortality rate among their children. And when this fact hit her, she became deeply troubled and upset—upset at herself for not telling the people she was a nurse and blaming herself for the death of little Rosey. "Perhaps if they had known about my skills they would have come to me sooner," she said.

Bending over the still, small form in the box, Thelma looked first at Rosey and then at the father. "If any of your other children ever get sick," she said, "please call me."

Shortly after that incident, the village council voted for Thelma to be in charge of the elected health leaders. These were paramedical people who reported serious illnesses and accidents by shortwave radio to Barrow. For Thelma this was the beginning of a tender and rewarding ministry among the Inupiat people of Wainwright and the surrounding area. And while she didn't realize it at first, the Lord had granted her the desire of her young heart—to live and work and nurse in a frontier community.

And then there was the third incident—an incident that nearly ended Don's ministry before it began.

7

Little Lost One

Like its neighbor the Arctic Ocean, the Arctic tundra is one of the world's most hostile environments. Harsh, treeless, and sparsely peopled, the tundra sits like a collar around northern Alaska, Canada, Greenland, and into European Russia and Siberia.

The uniqueness of the tundra is its very harshness—cold in winter with temperatures dipping to minus seventy degrees F. and soaring spasmodically and briefly to seventy and eighty degrees in summer. Then there is the permafrost. In summer only a thin surface of twelve to eighteen inches of soil becomes free of frost. Underneath is a concrete-hard layer of frozen ground where the temperature remains a constant minus thirty-two degrees F. In some places this permafrost reaches depths of 2,000 feet, thus preventing, during the season of the high climbing sun, any absorption of the melting runoff. This phenomenon causes the tundra to become a vast shallow marshland with tens of thousands of bogs, marshes, and water pockets that become ideal breeding spots for the infamous Alaskan mosquito. It also means that during the short growing season—June to August—the flat, undulating, soggy, mushy carpet of mosses and lichens becomes home to some of the most awe-inspiring plant life in the world.* With twenty-four hours of sunlight, much of the tundra erupts into a multicolored parade of oranges, yellows, whites, greens, purples, and reds. Plants like the fireweed, rhododendron, and fields of Arctic cotton grass spring forth. All this makes the tundra astonishingly beautiful, as well as an ideal breeding and feeding place for an equally fascinating parade of bird and animal life. Lemmings, foxes, wolves, bears, snowy owls, eider duck, ptarmigans—all these and much more live and die within an extraordinarily sensitive and fragile ecosystem.

One of the most exceptional mammals of the Alaskan tundra is the caribou. Traveling in herds that vary in size from 24,000 down to 230, caribou, like a living sea, invade the tundra each spring to calve and raise their young. For centuries the native peoples of the North have relied on the twice-yearly migrations (spring and fall) to supply them with food and skins for winter pants, gloves, socks, parkas, and bedding. To miss such a migration means great hardship; in some cases, it means death through starvation. The caribou migrations are also important to the coastal Inupiat, particularly in a year when seals or whales are scarce. And in 1959, the village of Wainwright hadn't taken a whale in more than four seasons.

Although Roy never once mentioned it, Don sensed the village was in short supply of meat. Yet this fact in no way hindered Roy from sharing a side of

---

*Not all tundra produces the same profusion. There are great stretches that contain only rocks, snow, and ice. Also, there is the eye of the beholder. Those accustomed to a rain forest view the tundra differently from those whose eyes view the blooming tundra in spring after seeing only polar landscape for ten months.

caribou with the newly arrived Websters. It was simply the Eskimo thing to do. Everyone shared, and as Don would soon learn, it would be impossible to outgive his new friends.

By about mid-February, the Websters had settled into the rhythm of village life. One of the unwritten rhythms of such a life asked that everyone who could should hunt and help supply fresh meat for the village. Don was happy, almost ecstatic, to realize he was expected to be a part of a hunt. Actually he had anticipated this and had purchased two rifles and had them shipped in along with his books and other supplies. These had now arrived, and he was eager to go on his first caribou hunt. There were always a few caribou who, for reasons unknown, remained on the tundra after the majority had migrated south. It was these Don went looking for on that day in February.

Wisely he chose a relatively "mild" day, about minus twenty degrees F. and a slight two- to three-knot wind. He dressed carefully—heavy underwear, wool shirt, tightly woven trousers, and parka. A few days earlier a neighbor had given Don a handsome pair of caribou socks. Thelma had not yet had the opportunity to learn how the Inupiat women sewed these for their menfolk.

The socks were long—up to his knee—with fur turned in against his skin. Over this, Don slipped on a pair of knee-high overboots made of caribou with the fur facing out (except for the soles). The last item was a new pair of caribou fur overmitts. He was careful to include a pair of wool undergloves as well. He did so with the memory of how unforgiving the Arctic can be to those who meet her cold unprepared.

The second week after Don's arrival in Wainwright, Roy's son Ben had taken him on his first caribou hunt. Ben rode the stanchions, that little platform at the back of the sled, and Don sat on top. In a great flurry of excitement, the dogs, after a shout from Ben as he released the snow hook, jerked at their traces and pulled the sled out over the snow-covered tundra. Don settled back to enjoy the ride and look at the countryside, but within a few minutes his glasses began to frost over.

Flipping off his overmitts that were on a harness over his shoulders, Don, with his hands now bare and exposed to the biting wind and extreme cold, reached in under his parka for the case to his glasses. But by the time he had reached into his pocket and taken out his case—in just those few seconds—the cold so numbed his fingers and sapped them of strength he was unable either to release the grip on his case or reach up to remove his glasses.

Immediately Don called for Ben's help. Halting the dogs, Ben set the snow anchor in place and came to Don's aid. Without a word of reproach for not wearing wool or felt undergloves, Ben literally pried Don's cold stiffened fingers from around the glass case. Next he removed Don's frosted glasses, put them in the case, and helped Don place his hands under his own armpits. Ben reminded Don that the warmer parts of the body— under the arms and in the groin—make excellent places to warm one's hands when they are cold.

With this memory in mind, Don made sure he had a pair of thick wool undergloves for his first solo hunting trip! He also made sure he had enough provisions to nourish himself out on the tundra. Into his Trapper Nelson packsack, he placed a small Primus stove and a pot for melting snow for tea and dried soup. He also packed a handful of Pilot Bread. This hardtack-like biscuit is one of the few positive legacies the avaricious and often ruthless whalers left the Eskimos.

Taking the main trail out of the village, Don walked south along the edge of the big stomach-shaped lagoon. It was still choked with ice and would be until spring thaw sometime in June. Don was in high spirits as he walked. For the first time in his life he was beginning to understand something of what it means to hunt in order to eat.

After about two miles, he left the trail that now had wound its way along the edge of the sea ice, climbed up over a large embankment, and headed inland across the tundra. The local gossip among the village hunters was that there was a small herd of caribou out near the DEW line radar station about three miles out on the tundra.

This was Don's first experience alone on the tundra. Like all Canadians, during his school days he had studied the flora and fauna of the northland and seen photos of its spectacular riot of spring color. But this was midwinter and it was difficult for him to envision this cold, barren, desolate land with its windswept snowdrifts piled high under the slopes and hills of the broken land ever capable of supporting life. But reason overcame his emotion of the moment and told him there was life out there—the hardy, nomadic caribou.

Don knew he was a novice and in a way knew he was challenging the Arctic without true Eskimo skills. For this reason he did everything by the book. Shortly after leaving the main trail, he took a compass reading and noted the time. It was 11:00 o'clock. Remembering that the sun set at about 6:00 P.M., he figured if he divided his time in half, he could hunt for about three hours and could make it back to the village before dark.

Walking at what he believed was a straight yet slightly angled direction into the wind, Don moved up and down the rolling plains. Whenever he could, he angled across the top of the hard pack snowdrifts rather than sink up to his knees in the small soft depressions. Finally, after about two hours, he came up over a slight rise and suddenly, there in front of him silhouetted against the gray sky, he spotted a small herd of eight or nine caribou. With his heart pounding so loudly he thought the caribou would surely hear, he knelt, unslung his rifle, and lined up a fine bull in his sights.

Untroubled by summer mosquitoes, blackflies, or botflies, the caribou grazed peacefully, pawing away the snow to get at the lichens and mosses. Handsomest in winter with their thick coat of rich cinnamon-brown with white necks and ventral manes, the animals stood motionless as they spotted Don. When nothing happened immediately, they believed the object on the horizon posed no danger and lowered their heads, resumed feeding, and moved upwind as they grazed.

But then the caribou heard a small popping sound. It was just a slight disturbance, but it startled them sufficiently that they ran out over the tundra for a few hundred yards. When they were satisfied there was no further danger, they resumed their grazing, confident that whatever had made such a sound had no real meaning to them.

Without the usual reference spots—a tree, pole, or rocks—on the barren snowscape, it was difficult for Don to judge exactly the distance between him and the caribou. He thought it to be about a quarter of a mile. An experienced hunter coming upon this herd would have at first stood still (Don did this), then quietly and slowly moved toward the caribou, letting them come to regard him as another caribou. Stalking the caribou in this manner allows a hunter to get surprisingly close and thus make a clean kill. Don followed no such pattern.

With his pulse banging in his head, he had allowed his excitement and anxiousness for a quarry to crowd out his good judgment. His first shot at such a distance succeeded only in causing the herd to run away. When they ran, this caused Don to commit one of several near fatal mistakes. He began walking after them and shooting whenever he came to within a quarter of a mile of the grazing herd.

For perhaps two hours he walked and shot and walked and shot, each time missing his target and pushing the herd farther and farther onto the tundra. So intense was he to get his first caribou that he lost all sense of time, until it was almost too late.

After his fourth or fifth failure at bagging a caribou, Don looked at his watch and suddenly came back to reality. It was almost 4:00 P.M.! Darkness would be upon him in two hours, and he had journeyed way beyond the halfway point. There was no way he could make it back to Wainwright before dark. Immediately he abandoned his thoughts about caribou hunting and started back toward the main trail. And this was where he made his second almost fatal mistake. He began to walk rapidly and started perspiring.

"To survive in the winter Arctic you must never perspire. To do so means that when you stop to rest and cool down, your perspiration will freeze you from the inside out." This had been a repeated warning from the instructor at Arctic Camp. Don knew it, and it made him all the more anxious because he was now perspiring. There was the further danger of freezing the tissue of his lungs if he were to breathe heavily.

Around dusk, after being exposed to the harsh elements for over eight hours, fatigue and dehydration were beginning to have their cumulative effect on Don's body. Newcomers to the Arctic often fail to recognize how much faster the body uses its store of calories in its battle against the cold. With his back to the wind, Don set up his Primus stove, melted some snow, and stirred in his dried soup. This, with several hard Pilot Bread biscuits, revived him. Being careful not to rest too long, he started out once again in the direction of the main trail. Fortunately the wind on the tundra was still relatively calm. Had there been a strong wind driving down the chill factor (some chill factors have been recorded as low as 100 degrees below zero), Don might well have perished long before now. However, the temperature had dropped to minus twenty-five degrees F.

To the novice, the tundra in winter appears like the surface of the moon—expressionless and without points of reference. To the Inupiat and those skilled in the lore of the Arctic, there are ample nooks and corners on the tundra to guide the traveler without the aid of a compass. They can even find their way back to camp by observing the imprint of the wind across the snowdrifts. Had Don known this, he may not have made his third mistake.

Shortly after his rest stop, he found and began to follow what he perceived to be the main trail back to Wainwright Village. For a long time the trail seemed exactly like the one he had taken earlier that morning before climbing up over that bank and turning inland over the tundra. But as he walked, he found the ground becoming more and more broken. He stumbled and slipped and slid more than he had in the morning, but he kept on walking, or rather groping, his way along.

Overhead the Arctic moon that sometimes becomes so bright one can almost hear its light, was hidden by a scattering of high cirrus clouds. There were stars—a multitudinous number—that blinked and twinkled through holes in the sky. And then suddenly, as if released from a secret cavern, long, pale, shimmering beams of the northern lights began to dance and wave across the cold night sky. Under different circumstances, it would have been a night to stand in awe at the wonder of God's creation. But on this night, Don was

in no mood to ponder the grandeur of this unique phenomenon. Fatigue was beginning to blur his mind and
as the northern lights began to fade, he was left with a
terrible feeling of helplessness and the startling realization that he wasn't on the trail at all. He was out on the
sea ice!

Up until this moment he hadn't allowed himself to
even consider the possibility of being lost. To be lost on
the tundra, alone, overnight, without shelter and food,
could end in only one way—death by freezing. For a
short moment, a surge of panic raced through his stomach and up his spine.

During his survival training both in Jungle Camp
and Arctic Camp, he had been warned about never
allowing himself to give in to the panic-urge. All his life
he had been a keen competitor. Whether as a boy playing hockey or struggling to learn the complexities of a
new language, he fought hard to win. Early in his life
and reinforced through his survival training, he had
learned that fear would hamper his ability to think, to
discriminate, and cause him to mistrust his own intui-
tion and feelings. Never was this fact more true than at
this moment. He was being forced to examine his feelings of being deceived. He truly believed the trail he
took was correct. How could he have been mistaken?

Yet he was. He would have to retrace his steps
back over the hard, uneven trail he had just come over
and try to find the correct trail. But what if he was
wrong? What if this trail could take him home? To go
off in the wrong direction would mean certain death.

By sheer force of will, Don held himself in check.
He refused to panic, to allow himself the release of his
own responsibility. Shaking the numbing fatigue from
his head, he began to reason. "If I am on the sea ice, it
means I am north of the village. I must begin by walking south. Turn around. I must go back."

Slowly and carefully making his way along what

he now believed to be the shoreline, Don began to experience all the things he had read about that happen to lost hunters. His legs, earlier so filled with energy and desire to carry him to the hunt, now ached and felt like straw. The weight of his pack and rifle slung across his back were barely noticeable that morning. Now they felt like lead weights that seemed to get heavier with every hump of broken ice he had to climb over. As he moved along the trail, his stumbling, often to his knees, became more frequent. Fatigued with heavy physical exertion, and drowsy with extreme weariness, his body demanded that he stop for rest. But his mind said no. Over and over he reminded himself that to stop would result in him becoming chilled, weariness would overtake him, and he would fall asleep and become entombed in ice from his perspiration.

Thus a battle emerged between Don's body and his mind. His body screamed for rest; his mind countered with, "You can do it. You've done it before. You must not give up. Remember in Jungle Camp on your survival exercise you got a second wind. You can do it now. Just keep moving. You're going to make it; you're going to make it. You must not give up." And Don stumbled and groped along the trail.

Then from out of his semi–delirium, he thought he saw a light. "That's got to be a beacon light from the village," he thought. "I must be close." But as he urged his body forward, he slipped down a depression and the light disappeared. "Is my mind playing little sadistic tricks?" thought Don. "I'll rest here for just a little bit, not more than two or three minutes, and try to climb up another rise and see if it will reappear."

Back in Wainwright, Thelma, now in what she believed to be her eighth month of pregnancy, busied herself during the day in an effort to take her mind off the thoughts of her young husband out on the tundra alone. When he had kissed her good-bye that morning and assured her he would be home before dark, by six, she hadn't worried too much. But it was now past six and very dark.

With her ears straining for his familiar footfall, Thelma tried to push aside the mounting anxiety collecting in her breast. By seven she was praying and pacing up and down in her little cabin. And when eight o'clock came and still her husband hadn't appeared, she threw on her parka and went to see Roy.

Without a single word to Thelma, Roy sprang from his chair, went outside, rang the school bell, and clicked on a beacon light high atop the antenna on the schoolhouse. Immediately, men from surrounding houses began running toward the direction of the school bell. "It's Webster," said Roy flatly. "He is out on the tundra. Hitch up your teams and get going." And that was that! Men began moving out in all directions. Thelma, comforted by the schoolteachers Ruth and Wilson Eckles, returned to her cabin to wait and pray and wonder if the child moving in her would have a father.

One man, Billy Patkutaq, who had become a quick friend to Don and Thelma, immediately drove his dog team out to the DEW line. Once there, Billy told his friend, the station chief, that Don was lost and asked if he could search for him in the bombadier. Billy knew this enclosed half-track snowmobile would make better time than conventional dog sleds. The station chief said yes, and both men took off in a cloud of white powdered snow.

Out on the tundra, Don, in a half dreamlike state, continued to do battle with his benumbed brain as he stumbled along trying to locate the source of the light. Was this the way of death? Did the brain succumb to one's fanciful wishes that somewhere out there in that cold black expanse someone was coming with a hot drink of tea? Someone was coming to rescue him and soon he'd have a nice warm place to rest? He had known of other lost hunters who told of strange optical effects, of rushing toward a beacon a quarter of a mile away that turned out to be a pile of rocks or a small bush. Breaking into his musings, Don's heart suddenly leaped. He again saw the light, only this time it was accompanied by a noise.

"It's the bombadier!" said Don to himself excitedly, but immediately it struck him that people were out looking for him and he experienced a kind of embarrassed ambivalence. Afraid of facing the ridicule of being lost, for a moment his pride superseded the reality of death he was facing moments before. "If they're out after me," he reasoned, "I can't be too far from the village. I won't let them know where I am. I'll walk in by myself."

But then, a wiser Don said to himself. "That's stupid. I'm exhausted. It doesn't matter how much fun they make of me, I've got to attract their attention. I won't be able to make it without their help."

With his priorities in order, Don unslung his rifle and fired three shots into the air. On the third shot, he saw the light swing around and come straight toward him.

Later that night, over steaming mugs of tea and hot chocolate, and while a relieved Thelma attended to his frostbitten nose and cheeks (his only injury), Don learned how he had been found. With great enthusiasm befitting Billy's warm Pentecostal faith, he explained how they had picked up Don's trail and tracked him for over twenty-five miles. "Webster was angling across the hard snow drifts. For this reason we had a hard time picking up his tracks. Fortunately he slipped into the little valleys enough times for us to pick them up again."

Don learned that he had been right in his belief that he was close to the village—about two miles when Billy picked him up. The trail he mistook for the main trail was an old dog sled trail. He had also been right in retracing his steps. The first light he had spotted was the beacon on top of the schoolhouse that was used to guide in the dog sleds after dark.

Don also learned the sober fact that had he been forced to remain on the tundra overnight, he most surely would have perished. As it was, he had been gone from home since ten that morning. It was 11:00 P.M. before the bombadier delivered him into Thelma's waiting and anxious arms.

To Don's surprise no one made fun of him, except that several days later as he went into the post office, some of the men smiled and good-naturedly pointed their chins in his direction. "Here comes *Tammagnaaraq,*" said one. Puzzled, Don later asked Roy what it meant.

"That means," said Roy with a half smile, "the Little Lost One."

"I suppose," said Don, "that will be my nickname forever."

"Yes," said Roy, "I suppose as long as the Inupiat drink hot tea and tell stories, you will be known as the Little Lost One, just as you are now known as *Webstarak*—Little Webster."

Thus Don's ordeal was over. There would be more, but perhaps with the coming of their first child they would face the most difficult of all ordeals.

8

The Happy House

Had there been a qualified obstetrician on staff at the small Barrow hospital in May 1959, the doctor, after examining Thelma, would have most certainly performed a cesarean section. But the attending doctor who had given Thelma a routine examination a month earlier was a geriatrician (a doctor who deals with the problems and diseases of the elderly), and had assured her he foresaw no problems. He was wrong. Here she was a month overdue and thirty long difficult hours into her labor and still unable to deliver. After the first several hours of labor, the doctor realized Thelma was in for a long and extremely difficult delivery. The baby's head wouldn't mold into the pelvis. To complicate matters, there was the danger of toxemia evidenced by a dramatic rise in her blood pressure. All this in a young woman who was with each contraction experiencing more pain than she had ever imagined possible.

Part of that pain went beyond the pain of the strong and continuous contractions. There was also the pain of being alone in Barrow. Except for a short visit in mid-April when he was puzzled over why the baby hadn't arrived, Don remained in Wainwright. They had mutually agreed it was best for him to remain in the village. Both were young and full of idealistic responsibility toward the work God had called them to and both were willing to make a sacrifice on behalf of this calling. Don had written in his journal of his own sense of loss and loneliness at seeing Thelma bounce over the tundra on her way out to the DEW line in the same bombadier that had rescued him. From there, an air force plane had taken Thelma and a young patient she was treating for tonsilitis to the Barrow hospital. Only in retrospect did Don realize the importance of being near his wife at such a dramatic moment. Thelma needed the calming reassurance of those she loved the most, but none were there and the contractions continued and continued and continued, all without the aid of an anesthetic.

Realizing his need for help, the attending doctor called in an obstetrician serving at the DEW line to take over. And then, at last, throughout a blanket of pain that tore into her very soul, Thelma delivered a girl. It was May 8, 1959.

A day later Don recorded in his journal these few words:

> 7:30 radio sked. John [the operator] tells me the good news. Girl born at 10:35 P.M. Wt. 9 lbs. ¾ oz.; length 22¾ inches. What a blessing, and what thanksgiving. Had breakfast with the Eckles who were around to hear the good news.

It was a euphoric moment for Don, a time to celebrate. God had given them their first child. But what he and Thelma didn't know was that this little girl (whom they named Mary Ellen after their mothers) was born with a condition known as craniostenosis. This simply meant little Mary Ellen was born with a premature fusion of the sutures between the bones of the skull. (This explained why Thelma had such a difficult delivery. At birth, the fontanels in a normal infant's skull tend to overlap, thus allowing for flexibility in the birth canal.) Without surgery, Mary Ellen's brain would have no space in which to grow. Unknown to Don and Thelma, this surgery should have taken place three to six months after birth.

For the moment, however, these two young people were aware only of being together as a family. Don wrote about how wonderful it was to be reunited with his wife, and in a typical husband comment, registered surprise at how small Mary Ellen was. (Thelma wished she had been several pounds lighter!) "For some reason," he wrote, "I was expecting Mary Ellen to have been about the size of a three-month-old."

Don's surprise at Mary Ellen's size soon gave way to wonder and awe at how a little life could bring such enrichment into their home. On May 21, just a day after Thelma and Mary Ellen arrived from Barrow, Don wrote in his journal: "I love my little daughter. Want to pick her up all the time." He did, however, qualify that statement with this last sentence: "Only midnight crying difficult."

And so began a new and expanded passage of learning for the Websters. Don and Roy pushed ahead on translation, and by mid-June, the two men had translated all the writings of John, except for Revelation. Don continued to struggle with the particular way Roy was translating, but resolved to go along with this until he himself had gained greater proficiency in the language.

On the other hand, Thelma's life changed dramatically. It seemed each day held some new and unexpected discovery of how different it was to live in the Arctic. She began to make daily rounds, visiting, nursing, giving immunization shots to babies, treating cuts and colds and ear infections, of which there were plenty. For the most difficult cases, she consulted, via shortwave radio, with the doctor in Barrow. All this she worked around caring for Mary Ellen and serving hot tea and some of her baked goods to the several visitors that came each day. In the evenings, while Don continued to study and after he had helped her with the dishes, she indulged herself by sketching and painting with water colors. At first she did this for her own enrichment, but when Don began working on reading materials, primers, and a new hymnbook for the Inupiat church, she used her skills to add color and interest to the books.

Thelma used her skills and considerable character in coping not only with the public relations demands of being a translator's wife, but also with learning to handle the harsh demands of an Alaskan frontier. She discovered, to her dismay, that even though the calendar said July or August, washed sheets and diapers could freeze solid and snap in the wind like brittle kindling wood. She also learned how much she had taken for granted: such plain and ordinary items as washtubs, hot and cold running water, and an electric washing machine. Back home in Ontario she had gone about the usual Monday morning wash without too much thought, except that the hour or so she spent performing this necessary but routine task was somehow not related to the more important issues of living. Not so in Wainwright. Just to procure enough water for washing and drinking became one of the all-consuming functions of their daily lives. In a letter home Thelma wrote:

We collect snow from the nearest drift and melt it down for washing. Our drinking water is taken from ice blocks that Don cuts from a nearby fresh water lake. This, like the coal we use to heat our house, is hauled in by dog sled.

What Thelma failed to mention was that with the arrival of Mary Ellen, washday became a three- to four-day project. It took a full day just to melt enough snow to get enough water to use in their gas-powered washing machine. A half-day was used to wash the diapers and other things, and one to two days more to dry them. Since they couldn't be hung outside, the diapers were pinned on wires near the ceiling. And in this twelve- by fifteen-foot house with its tiny sleeping loft, the hanging diapers hit Don just about in the middle of his forehead.

Not all the things Thelma learned during those first few months had to do with physical endurance. She made the interesting discovery that since there were fewer people to talk with, she had more time to pray. This heightened awareness of fellowship with God brought about a new understanding of what it means to "walk (live) not after the flesh (human approval, or social preoccupation), but after the Spirit" (Romans 8:4).

Thelma's earlier dreams had been to work in some romantic northern outpost. Now that she was here, she discovered Arctic living wasn't as "romantic" as she had once thought. Nonetheless, she was strangely at peace with herself even without electricity, proper indoor plumbing, and having to maintain a considerable nursing practice while being wife, mother and hostess.

As Don struggled with the complexities of the Inupiat language, he discovered many interesting linguistic features. For example, the Inupiat never use *when* in reference to the future. It is always *if*, "if such and such a person comes back from the hunt . . ." He deduced this had evolved because the Inupiat live continually on the thin edge of physical danger.

Don also learned how much hard work was involved in hunting seals and other game. On several occasions he accompanied the men out on the ice only to find himself crawling over the cold uncomfortable frozen sea on his stomach in an effort to stalk a seal that slept warily beside an open lead. He also learned about the respect one must pay to a dead animal and about the correct way to handle the carcass.

On one occasion while duck hunting with a crew of men, Don noticed a dead duck propped up in the stern of the boat. "It can't be a decoy," he thought, "the duck is partly hidden." With his usual jocularity and in an effort to be one with the men, Don lifted the head of the dead duck and imitated the duck's quacking sound. Immediately, one of the older men, with a sternness Don hadn't experienced before, said simply, "Don't do that!"

Don was immediately aware he had made a breach of Inupiat culture. He would come to understand that the always practical Eskimo believed an animal allowed himself to be killed and would become reborn and allow himself to be killed again, only if the hunter treated him with respect. Part of that respect meant that the carcass must be given a drink of water to quench the animal's fiery thirst. It was also believed that if a hunter were extremely offensive, the entire community could be affected with loss of food.

Don also learned how important it was for marine mammals to be shown respect. If, for example, a hunter killed a seal, some part of the seal must be thrown back into the sea. This was particularly true when a boy made his first kill. In this case, the bones of the seal were gathered up and thrown back into the sea at the very spot the seal had been killed. The reason was simple: to keep on good terms with the seal's soul. By keeping this ritual the seal would then return again and again to be killed by the same hunter. Uppermost in every hunter's mind was the steady supply of food to support himself, his family, and friends. It was therefore necessary always to maintain a profound respect for nature and the animals that gave him sustenance.

Later on, about midnight of the day he had imitated the quacking sound, Don quietly asked the older man what he had done wrong earlier. For a long time the man remained silent. At first Don thought he was going to ignore his question. At last the man spoke, his voice soft and subdued. "When I was young, my father told me we should never play with dead animals like that." And that was all he said.

In a conversation about this incident with Roy several days later, Don noticed Roy become more disturbed than he had ever seen him. "There is nothing wrong with rituals and ceremonies," said Roy. "We have the blanket toss to celebrate the end of a successful whale hunt. It's at this time everyone can share and feast on *muktuk* and whale flipper. And even some of our taboos have their origin in keeping the food chain alive. Our older men told us it was once a taboo for any one hunter to kill more than five wolves for their pelts. And in summer when our women and children found a cache of *utkuk* (small potatoes) that little tundra mice had stored for winter, it was a taboo to take all the roots. The taboo said you must leave enough for the mice to survive the winter, then the following summer you will have more roots from the same mice. But this man you told me about is clearly filled with superstition. There is no place for one who knows Christ as his Lord to behave superstitiously. I will make a point of dropping around and visiting him."

Yet in spite of these hunting taboos that were considered superstitious by Roy and the Christian community, some taboos were woven into the very fabric of what it means to be both Eskimo and Christian. For as long as any Inupiat remembered, they have held in disfavor any man who boasted about his prowess as hunter. It was thought such egocentric behavior would be offensive to an animal's spirit, and the hunter would be prevented from catching any further animals.

The concept that egocentric, boastful or prideful people in some way hurt themselves and those they live with found support in Christian teaching. Little by little as Inupiat believers became aware that God hated displays of arrogance or pride or boasting of whatever sort, the old hunting taboo took on new meaning. Now, rather than being concerned about offending the animal spirit, believers are concerned about offending the Spirit of the living God. Through a maturing of their faith, many realize that in all things, hunting included, they must rely upon the living God to help them. And since it is He who guides and provides their food, what reason do they have to boast?

In theory, Don knew this concept to be true. But it took an incident on a caribou hunting trip to show him how perfectly the Inupiat have integrated this in daily practice.

Traveling in Roy's motor launch and pulling a skin boat behind, Don, Roy, and three other men ploughed forty miles inland up a narrow river. When the launch had gone as far as it could go in the shallow river, the men beached it on a sandbar and transferred to the skin boat. When they had traveled upriver several more miles, the men decided to set out the seine net and fish. In the process of coming into shore, Don prematurely jumped out of the boat and fell into the water up to his armpits.

While it was the end of August, the weather was still cool and it was decided Don should return to the launch to dry out his clothes. And that's when all the excitement happened. Sitting with nothing but a blanket around him, Don, to his astonishment, spotted seven caribou coming out across the sandbar. With his heart in his mouth and fumbling to keep the blanket wrapped around him, he grabbed his rifle and began firing. In a moment, all seven caribou lay on the sandbar. It was a moment of intense pride in having provided such bounty for himself and the village.

Like a young child eager to show his parents his first "A" on an exam, Don could hardly wait until Roy and the men returned. When at dusk they finally did, there wasn't the slightest gesture of surprise or expression of how well this *taanik* (white man) had done on his first real caribou hunt. In an offhanded way, Roy said flatly, "We'll skin them out in the morning," and the young translator was left to ponder the ways of the Inupiat.

At the same time, the Inupiat pondered the ways of the *taanik*. In August, Thelma cared for a young girl while the girl's mother went to the hospital. When it came time to retire, the girl was astonished to discover the rumor about the *taaniks* was true. These strange white people changed clothes to go to bed!

There was one strange *taanik* practice that gave a happy surprise to everyone who visited the Websters' cabin. By mid-August the walls in the cabin were finally dry and the drab gray paint was ready to be covered over with something clean and bright. Since there were so few days of sunshine, the Websters wanted to create an illusion of eternal spring. This they did by painting the windowless wall a bright sunburst yellow, the opposite walls a bright green, and the ceiling white. Thus when visitors passed through the dark outer sheds and opened the door to the newly painted room, the unexpected brightness practically took their breath away. Overnight the Wainwright Inupiat nicknamed it "The Happy House." And by the first week in September, The Happy House was made even happier by the arrival of the North Star.

Transporting more than 300,000 items of food, building materials, and other supplies, the North Star freighter, operated by the Bureau of Indian Affairs, is a lifeline for most of the isolated settlements along Alaska's North Slope. As the freighter slowly made its way up the coast, the air was thick with excitement.

Each night for more than a week the Websters tuned their shortwave radio to the North Star's frequency. In a flat, unemotional voice they heard the radio man ask about weather conditions and assorted details about landing the items designated for that particular village. Since there were no docking facilities, the ship's cargo had to be slung over the side and lowered into little *umiaks* and old World War II landing barges that bobbed up and down in the cold water like corked bottles.

As the days passed, the voice on the ship's shortwave radio came to have an irresistible attraction to the Websters. After eating mostly beans for eight months, the anticipation of at long last being able to have fresh eggs, cheeses, and vegetables captivated their attention.

Finally the voice said: "Wainwright Village, this is North Star. Do you read me? Want to make contact. We are in Kotzebue. We have two more days of unloading, then on to Point Hope. We estimate Wainwright Village in five days."

And then on September 4, 1959, the North Star gave a short whistle blast and dropped anchor a mile offshore from Wainwright Village. For a full day the ship lay at anchor, unable to off-load its cargo into the eager *umiaks* and barges. It was just too stormy.

It was hard to know who was more disappointed—the adults or children. Adults were used to disappointment, but the children found waiting for their annual treat unbearable. This treat came from someone the children thought was the most famous and important man aboard the North Star. His name was Cecil "Moe" Cole,★ the North Star's Second Officer. This affable bear of a man had over the years given out candies, oranges, toys, and other delicacies to the children in each village. And the children were just as eager for the storm to subside as their parents.

At long last, on September 6, at 10:00 A.M., the unloading began to get underway. Everything, including school, closed down and for the next twenty-one hours, every able-bodied man, woman, and child worked all that day and through the night until 7:00 A.M. the next day, unloading the barges and carrying the items to the respective homes. Besides being a happy time, it was a time to pick up extra money for longshoring.

Then almost without notice, the North Star hoisted its anchor and steamed off out of sight. It would be another twelve months before the village would again have contact with the outside world in such a dramatic way.

Of that moment, Don wrote:

It was a joyous time. Everyone happily worked, eager to see the things they had ordered twelve months before. The ship was rushed constantly, fighting against ice and freeze-up. The Coast Guard ice-breaker North Wind accompanied the North Star.

After eating all those beans, we were almost overcome to have something fresh. It was a delicious experience to bite into a raw onion.

For the moment, the Websters had enough food to last through another harsh Alaska winter. Their house was now comfortable, and they were enjoying their

★As of this writing, Cecil "Moe" Cole is Captain of the North Star II.

ministry among the people of Wainwright. In reality this was a lull before the storm. Actually, it was the lull before three storms.

9

The Revival

On a November day in 1960, two men passed as strangers in the dark. The plane that was to take Roy Ahmaogak out to a special Presbytery meeting, brought in Mr. M. M. Butterfield—the revivalist!

Ten months after the Websters began their Bible translation ministry among the Inupiat, the Assemblies of God church sent in fifty-year-old, two-fisted Cecilia Piper to begin her own brand of mission activity among the people of Wainwright Village. Both Roy and Don were a little unhappy over the prospects of another mission work. Roy pointed out that Wainwright had been a Presbyterian preserve for over fifty years and that the more casual and flamboyant ministry of this church would confuse and divide the people. "After all," said Roy, "there are only 250 people in Wainwright. They will draw the people away from our own Presbyterian church."

The always practical and frugal Don agreed with Roy. He felt the money needed to support a missionary and church building could be better spent in an area where there was no Gospel witness. Yet, because he represented a nonsectarian mission board himself, Don couldn't take sides. "If a new work gets started," he reasoned, "they'll need the New Testament just as much as the believers in the Presbyterian church."

Thus in November 1960, a week after the Presbyterians held their special preaching mission, the new Assemblies of God church began theirs.

In his journal, Don noted the Presbyterian meetings hadn't been marked by an overabundance of spiritual ardor. "Just a few older people who came forward to publicly declare their desire to rededicate their lives to the Lord."

Don's remark about the *older* people responding was no idle scribble. Ever since his arrival in 1958, Don had noted a decided lack of spiritual interest among the young people in Wainwright. "There is little talk about the Word of God in their hearts," said Don. And in a letter written in March 1960 to acquaint their praying and supporting friends with what Wainwright Village was like, he had written:

> Wainwright is a conglomerate of mostly houses haphazardly grouped around the government schoolhouse on the rim of the Arctic Ocean. The forty-five small houses accommodate 250 Inupiat Eskimos. The Pentecostal missionary, school teaching family and ourselves complete the citizenry—along with 300 sled dogs. The houses are all frame type; a few are built from tundra sod. These coastal Eskimos never did build snow igloos like the Canadian Eskimos.
>
> Our "shopping center" consists of the native co-op store. The rest of the "business section" with the exception of one small store is in private homes. We do have a coffee shop and two movie theatres. The latter businesses are of questionable influence.
>
> Since last spring we were raising three sled dogs and then an epidemic of distemper hit the village. Now we have only one left.

The Word is being preached and I know it is bearing fruit among the older people. However, the younger people, while they come to services, seem to be Gospel hardened. *Please pray especially for them.*

That March letter, with just a touch of despair over the spiritual apathy of Wainwright's young people, was followed by another letter dated November 19, 1960. More a bulletin than a letter, it fairly exploded with joyous enthusiasm.

Hallelujah! Praise Jehovah! Amen! Revival has come to Wainwright. For the past ten days we have been exulting in the incomparable joy of spiritual revival. Except for four or five men, every Inupiat in our village of 250 over the age of sixteen has given his heart to the Lord or been revitalized in his faith. The young people have been particularly touched. We know this is a definite answer to your prayers as well as ours. How did it happen?

How indeed did it happen? On the Monday night after the visiting Presbyterian preacher had concluded the special preaching mission in Roy's church, M. M. Butterfield and his team began their special preaching mission in the Pentecostal church. Unsure as to how closely he should associate himself with this new group, Don decided to stay home that first night. He did, however, send Thelma! When Thelma returned home, she was visibly upset.

"The preacher was a typical fiery evangelist," she reported. "A lot of people came down the aisle weeping and carrying on. I don't know what to make of it. For me it's just too much hullabaloo. Tomorrow night you're going."

And Don did.

True to his wife's report, Tuesday night was a carbon copy of Monday night. Don was surprised to see many of the village young people going forward when the invitation was given and weeping as they knelt at the altar.

When the service concluded, Don had a mild encounter with Cecilia Piper. In spite of their theological differences, this energetic woman had become a warm friend to the Websters. "I find all this to be quite unbiblical," said Don smiling. "The Scriptures clearly teach that any gathering in the name of the Lord should be done 'decently and in order.' Furthermore, a meaningful spiritual experience does not have to be extraordinary to be a true work of God's Holy Spirit."

Cecilia, who knew Don could easily back her into a theological corner, countered with, "Come to the after-service and see how the Spirit of God is working in the lives of these young people. You'll be impressed."

And Don was impressed. Over two years had passed since he first came to Wainwright. In all that time not one Inupiat had displayed the kind of emotion he was now witnessing. As each young person (mostly teenagers) stood to tell how they personally felt about Jesus Christ, the usual stoic mantle dropped away and they wept openly.

This was a new side to the Inupiat people he had never seen, nor expected to see. But there was more. As the week of meetings in the Assembly of God church continued, the young people who went forward each evening for salvation or rededication met together the following day, on their own initiative, to sing and pray and to read the Scriptures (the only Scriptures were those in English).

This quite overwhelmed Don. He was delighted to see an answer to his prayer, but disappointed this new awakening hadn't happened under his own ministry. He was also concerned about the somewhat "eccentric" behavior causing a division between the young (thirty on down) and older people. Most of the older people were happy to see their young people "turned on" for the Lord, but weren't happy about it happening outside the established Presbyterian church. All this happened between Monday and Saturday. And then came Sunday.

Before Roy left for his Presbytery meeting, he had arranged for the Sunday morning worship service to be conducted by one of the elders. Roy then asked Don if he would be in charge of the less formal evening service.

In anticipation of what could happen in the soon-to-be inaugurated Pentecostal church, the visiting preacher had spoken on the biblical understanding of what it means to be filled with the Spirit (from a traditional Calvinistic point of view). In the afternoon, as Don thought and prayed about what he would say that evening, he struggled with at least three difficult tensions. First, he wondered what form his remarks should take. Would it be helpful to build on what the visiting Presbyterian preacher had spoken about? Next, he struggled with how to involve the older people. Some had expressed interest in what was happening to their young people but were confused and wanted to know how they too could be a part of such spiritual manifestations.

The third tension centered around how to preserve the unity of the Presbyterian membership, between young and old, and between those influenced by Pentecostalism who held a number of theological views different from the more conservative Presbyterians. It was imperative for community survival that there be harmony in the village. They were hunters and depended upon each other for help.

There was yet another concern for Don, though not as worrisome as the others. Since there was to be a service in the Pentecostal church at the same time as theirs, he wondered if many people would come. But when he took his seat on the platform and looked out over the congregation, his last worry dissolved. Almost every seat was filled. "Perhaps they are loyal Presbyterians after all," he thought.

With slow, carefully measured words, Don through the aid of an interpreter, Peter Tagrook, explained that revival was not the private preserve of Pentecostalism but available to any Christian who would surrender his all to the Lord. "In its simplest terms," said Don, "revival occurs among God's people when they begin to take seriously what God has told them in His Word. And to be filled with the Spirit of God means we depend upon God's Holy Spirit to lead and direct us in all the ordinary things we do in life. If we hunt, or fish, or teach school, or visit the sick, or work in a store, it is what He has chosen for us to do. If we ask Him to lead and direct us in our everyday lives, we are being filled with God's Spirit."

Don continued to talk for a few more minutes and stressed that no Christian can be Spirit-filled with unconfessed sin in his life. He also explained that for the Spirit of God to be evidenced in a person's life didn't necessarily mean there had to be a visible or spectacular demonstration. Don talked about how the Spirit works quietly in a person's life in subtle ways and that one of the great works of the Spirit is to help the believer *endure* and have power to *go through* and *overcome* various kinds of trials and suffering. (Within seven months, he would dramatically experience the reality of what he now was expounding as theory.) He concluded his remarks with one last thought.

"Most of us first approached God by taking simple baby steps. Remember, God always stands ready and willing to meet us with whatever degree of dedication we are willing to give Him. If there are those who would like to come to the front of the church to pray, please feel free to do so."

Don then closed the meeting with prayer, sat down, and began to pray silently. Almost before he had rested his face in his hands to pray, he heard the scuffing of chairs. The noise came from members of the small choir to the left of the platform and young people getting up and coming forward. Next, one of the leading elders of the church stepped up, and as he knelt to pray, he waved an open invitation with his arm for all the rest of the congregation to come, too. Before Don knew what was happening, the entire church, with the exception of three men, came forward and began pouring out their hearts to God in audible prayer.

At first this spontaneous, simultaneous talking to God by seventy people frightened Don. After all, this wasn't his church. He was really only helping out during Roy Ahmaogak's absence. And as a member of SIL, he shouldn't have even been taking part in clerical activities. But then he thought, "What is there to be afraid of? If the Spirit of God is at work, then I'll move with Him." With that, Don also got down on his knees and began to confess his own reservations about how the Spirit would work.

For the next fifteen to twenty minutes, everyone prayed at once, and then little by little the praying subsided and finally stopped. When the praying ended, the singing and testifying began. "I just feel as if wings have come down from heaven and lifted up my heart," one man said. "I want to be a different kind of man than I was before I came to this meeting." Others asked forgiveness of some of their friends for hurting them or talking about them behind their backs. On and on it went, until when some of the younger children began to get restless and babies began to cry the meeting ended. Later Don wrote:

You can't begin to imagine the superb thrill of over

seventy believers of one mind simultaneously talking to God unless you have shared the experience. Following the prayer, we sang, testified, and praised God. About 11:00 P.M. we felt constrained to terminate the meeting because of the presence of a number of smaller children. But we were sorry to leave the House of God. This was Christian fellowship at its fullest and finest. Words fail to express our overwhelming gratitude to our blessed Savior.

With this unprecedented experience in the Presbyterian church, the whole village was now involved in a spirit of revival. And true to the words of the Apostle Paul in his letter to the Ephesian Church, all the Inupiat believers—Pentecostal and Presbyterian—while remaining loyal to their denomination, were patient and gentle with each other and made every effort to maintain the unity of the Spirit and the bond of peace.

One of the principle reasons for the unity in Wainwright came through a man who hadn't even witnessed or taken part in any of the revival meetings. That man, of course, was Roy Ahmaogak. When he returned on the Monday following the outpouring of prayer and testimony the night before, many in his congregation were worried about how he would respond. Just about the time he had slipped out of his parka after riding in on a dog-drawn sled from where the plane had landed, a delegation of elders knocked at his door. Shortly after the elders had finished explaining what had happened while he was away, Don arrived to add his influence to keep the village from any spiritual cross-purposes. After the elders and Don had exhausted their explanations about all that happened, they waited for Roy's comment. Nothing on his face betrayed either displeasure or approval of what the men had told him. Yet when he spoke, each knew again why God had called Roy to be their pastor.

When men make choices, they make them out of

their character. Immature men choose things that are self-seeking. On that day, however, Roy showed that a good man, a mature man, a courageous man, chooses for the sake of what is good and noble and best for the whole community. "I agree we should not polarize our community. Also it seems that I have indeed returned to a village that is different from what I left. What has happened is outside my experience, but I will wait and see how God will use this new thing."

Of those days, Don wrote: "I don't know if I ever lived closer to heaven on this earth."

This was also true for a great many others who continued to experience a sense of euphoria all through that winter. For many who remember those days, however, it was more than just a time of warm, fuzzy feelings. People continued to experience the Holy Spirit convicting them of sin and leading them to righteousness.

One of those was a young man who worked on the DEW line military base. Everyone knew he was notorious for his drinking, stealing, and womanizing. One afternoon while running his dog team out to the coal mine, an inner voice spoke to him as plain as an audible voice. It seemed, he said later, to be like the voice of his dead grandfather who said: "You go back to the village and get your heart right with the Lord."

Whatever happened that afternoon on the tundra, the young man immediately returned to the village and joined himself to a group of young people who were having a mid-afternoon Bible study. He did get his heart right before the Lord, just as the voice commanded!

Never in its history had any event so captivated the attention of the people of Wainwright, except perhaps when someone raced through the village yelling, *"Agvik! Agvik!"* (bowhead, bowhead). And that's ex-

actly what happened five months after the revival and
following a special day of prayer. A mighty bowhead
was sighted and subsequently taken. It was the first
whale the people of Wainwright had harvested since
1955. Just as when the North Star dropped anchor, every available person came out to help and watch the
excitement. Some of the younger people had never seen
a whale or helped with getting the immense carcass up
onto the ice for butchering. And when with block and
tackle the bowhead was dragged out of the water onto
the ice, it took about seventy people with long flensing
knives, working steadily for thirty-six hours, to butcher
the huge mammal and cart off the heavy chunks of meat
and blubber. Also, for the first time in over five years,
the village would spend two to three days celebrating
this great event with a *nalukatak* or blanket toss. Traditionally the blanket toss was celebrated to mark the end
of a successful whale hunt. And on this April day in
1961, the village had a double reason to celebrate.

Many in the village attributed this whale (some
called it a "whale of faith") directly to the Lord. Others
agreed and said that through the revival the Lord had
granted His favor upon the village and they were
blessed because they had maintained love and unity between the two churches.

Clearly this was a time to celebrate, and the people
in Wainwright dressed in their finest parkas, feasted on
muktuk and whale flipper and drank gallons of hot tea.
The feasting, which went on all afternoon and into the
evening, was interspersed with the famous blanket toss.

In reality, the blanket toss is not done with a blanket at all but a hand-sewn walrus hide. With a dozen or
so men gripping the edges of the "blanket," they flip a
young person into the air. Each time the person lands on
the blanket, he is flipped higher and higher into the air.
And all the time the surrounding crowd cheers and

sucks in their breath with appropriate "oh's" and "ah's."

When the celebration was over, the *umialik* (the man who owned the big skin boat and had financed the crew that took the whale and therefore played host to the *nalukatak*) called for the dividing of the meat. With this open-handed display of generosity, the *umialik* (literally, captain or rich man) gained prestige. To be sure, the *umialik* and the whaling crew received the largest and choicest parts; yet all benefited from the harvest. That day everyone was happier than he remembered being for a long time. Everyone, except perhaps Don and Thelma. Oh, they were happy that all the ice cellars were crammed full of food against the hard cold of a long winter. And they were still basking in the afterglow of the revival. It was just their concern for little Mary Ellen.

In November, Thelma had noticed Mary Ellen's right eye was becoming crossed. She thought perhaps it was nothing more than a muscle spasm, but when Dr. Walter, Wainwright's itinerant doctor, examined her, he suggested they take her immediately to Anchorage for tests.

Dr. Walter, a kindly Christian gentleman, had understood the Websters' concern to have their daughter under proper medical care as quickly as possible. He also had understood the Websters' limited finances and accordingly arranged for Thelma to act as her American-born daughter's escort to Anchorage. Under a provision of the United States Social Services program, such persons with low incomes were provided free transportation to medical care. However, it took until January 1961, two months after his examination, before all the administrative details were worked out. Dr. Walter was also sensitive to Thelma's need for emotional warmth and support. Unfortunately, the attending woman pediatrician in Anchorage who had conducted two days of tests on Mary Ellen lacked Dr. Walter's empathetic sensitivity.

"I understand you have another daughter," said the doctor.

"Yes," said Thelma, "Rebecca Lee (Becky) was born eleven months after Mary Ellen."

"Were there complications with this delivery?"

"No, not at all."

"And did you think to question why your second daughter's delivery was normal and your first wasn't? Didn't you think this was unusual?"

"No, I'm afraid I didn't," said Thelma. "Becky weighed only 5 lbs. 10 oz. and Mary Ellen was well over 9 lbs. I thought this was the reason and that Mary Ellen just wouldn't mold into the birth canal."

"Exactly right," said the doctor. "And the reason for this was because the lateral sections of your daughter's cranium were fused together. In normal children these plates tend to overlap during birth and allow for easier molding into the birth canal. However, now this premature fusing has kept the bones of the head from expanding as they should, and it's this brain pressure that's causing the eye to cross.

"But of course that is past history. We now have to concern ourselves with the surgical correction of this problem. The usual procedure in such cases is to operate three to six months after birth. As you know, the bones are much more elastic at that time and the operation less complicated. Your daughter is already past the age where the operation will be 100 percent successful and each month's delay means a greater danger of mental retardation.

"The procedure—a craniotomy—is to remove two strips of bone at the back of the skull. This empty space will give the brain room to grow" . . . and on and on went the lengthy explanation. Thelma needed to know—wanted to know—more details about Mary Ellen's medical problems, but the shock of suddenly and unexpectedly learning her daughter needed major surgery, and told to her in such an unfeeling and casual manner, was almost more than she could bear. But the doctor had more.

"I would like to operate immediately, but your daughter has some further complications that will require a season of medication. Our tests reveal she has a chronic ear infection that has impaired her hearing and she also has a primary lesion of TB."

"TB?" gasped Thelma.

"Yes, TB," said the doctor. "In all probability she picked it up from some older person in Wainwright who visited you in your home or when you visited the sick. You said you were a nurse, and there is TB in the village. You do visit the sick, don't you?"

"Yes, yes, I do," said Thelma weakly.

"Also," continued the doctor, "your daughter has some inflammation around the toenails, probably in-grown toenails, and . . ."

Almost overcome with the enormity of what she was hearing, Thelma wanted to scream, "Enough! Enough! The sky has fallen in on me. How much more do you think I can take? I don't believe she's retarded. Why do you put such doubts in my mind? Don't you realize this girl has never been outside our little house? How can your sophisticated puzzle tests apply to her? Anyway, why have you been so calloused and tactless?" Thelma wanted to say all these things, but didn't. God's inner strength allowed her to remain silent. Retreating to her own private world, she hardly heard the doctor's further instructions about medication for the TB and that they should set a surgical date three months hence.

As the two women walked out of the consultation room into the waiting room where Don held his second daughter, the doctor stopped to observe her.

"Is this your other daughter?" she asked.

"Yes," said Thelma, "this is Becky."

"Well, how nice. At least you have one nice normal child."

10

Living Without Answers

The operation was supposed to have taken place in March of 1961, but governmental regulations and a change in the U.S. Social Health Services programs delayed the Websters' plans. Finally, a full six months after the initial testing that determined she would need an operation, little Mary Ellen was wheeled into surgery. It was 8:00 A.M., June 28, 1961.

At that moment, Don and Thelma were taking up their silent vigil in the waiting room, each lost in reflection. Thelma eyed words in an attempt to read but found her mind racing over recent events—the vague uneasiness on the south-bound flight that the operation would still have to be performed; the blow at hearing the verdict; the battery of preoperation tests, all so bewildering to their small, uncomprehending daughter; the upsetting moments on the afternoon before when Mary Ellen had cried with such fright during the blood test; finally settling her in her crib with her teddy bear, and then slipping out of the room when she was momentarily distracted by the baby in the crib next to hers; that last fleeting glance of her big blue eyes and blond curly hair . . .

Don's mind went back to January. He had just returned from the hospital in Anchorage with Mary Ellen, and after getting over the hard shock of his daughter's physical condition, he determined to meet God in a new way. Prior to the revival and in keeping with his training as a conservative theologian, Don had clearly defined for himself how he believed God should and could manifest Himself. There was seldom room for any other biblical interpretation beyond what his theological system allowed. Thus, when he witnessed firsthand an obvious outpouring of the Spirit of God that didn't fit his theological grid, he began to reexamine his theology.

Doctrines, after all, as he once heard Dr. Nida express it, "are man's imperfect attempts to express in human terms a far greater reality involving the action and person of the Supernatural." While Don, by his own admission, tended to be a bit dogmatic about his own piety, he was honest enough to realize that he, like all of Christendom, "sees through a glass darkly." He also knew, albeit slightly at first, that God works through culture, history, and contemporary events, and that He sometimes pours new wine into new wineskins—which is to say what every thoughtful believer in Jesus Christ has always known—God is unpredictable!

Knowing all this, and being committed to Scripture and with a passion for vital contact with God, Don and Thelma set aside each Monday for prayer and fasting. With care and humility, Don spent part of those Mondays closely examining all the Scriptures he could find that dealt with healing. While the spiritual high of the revival experience had been swept away in the face of Mary Ellen's problem, Don and Thelma were open to new ways for God to work.

The Websters had seen God work in unusual and unexpected ways during the revival, and in a unique way this had prepared them for what they were now facing. If God worked on behalf of the Inupiat people by bringing so many of them to faith, surely God would perform a miracle on their daughter's behalf. After all, they reasoned, isn't a life lived by expectant faith the very substance that gives meaning to one's spiritual union with God?

While this reasoning is true, it is equally true that spiritual growth comes *through* the struggle with crises and pain. And in a way quite beyond their expectation, God involved most of the believers in Wainwright in this crisis struggle. Wrote Don:

> On January 29, we had a special day of prayer for our little girl. All our Eskimo friends united with Thelma and me to pray and ask God to touch Mary Ellen's body with His healing power. We believe that this is not only a special time of testing, but also a special time of opportunity for God to perform a miracle.
>
> We know God can work. We are still enjoying the results of last November's revival. There is a new atmosphere of unity and love in the village plus a keenness among the believers for the deeper things of God. Interestingly, even one of the movie houses has closed down. It used to be possible to see twelve movies in a single week. Now the one remaining theater only shows three or four films each week. We have much cause for rejoicing and thanksgiving.

Thelma, as well as Don, discovered a new confidence in prayer. Called on to treat fevers, colds, earaches, and other related problems, Thelma began praying more and giving fewer penicillin shots with surprisingly greater results than she had had in the past. On one occasion, she was called to treat a boy for a severe pain in his lower abdomen. After prayer for wisdom, she diagnosed the pain as a ruptured appendix. Unable to contact the doctor to confirm her suspicions, she arranged for a special flight to the Barrow hospital. Later, when the hospital confirmed her diagnosis, Thelma thanked God for giving her the wisdom to act as swiftly and decisively as she did on behalf of the boy. All this seemed to be one more evidence that God was indeed going to touch Mary Ellen with His healing power.

And on one particular Monday night after the Websters had finished their fast and were preparing to retire, an unusual sense of expectancy came over Don. As was their custom, Don and Thelma normally prayed in bed. It was generally too cold in the upstairs sleeping loft to remain outside the blankets. But on this Monday night, Don experienced an unexplainable buoyancy of spirit and knelt beside his bed and prayed, quite oblivious to the cold.

As he prayed, it seemed the Spirit of God prompted him to pray for the healing of Mary Ellen's eye.* At first he hesitated. "Lord, I don't want to put You to the test." But at the moment he hesitated, the strange sense of joy and buoyancy he had experienced as he came to prayer, left him. Finally, to regain his joy, Don said simply, "Lord, I claim healing for Mary Ellen's eye. And I thank You for it in Jesus' name. Amen."

"That moment," said Don, "was perhaps one of the most sublime I have ever known." Lost in the aura and expectancy of what God was going to do, he

---

*In an effort to strengthen Mary Ellen's weak eye, the doctor recommended she wear a patch over her good left eye. But Mary Ellen did what any normal eighteen- to nineteen-month-old child would do—she tore it off. When Thelma put an old pair of frame glasses on Mary Ellen with the patch attached to the lens over the good eye, she cried because she couldn't see.

climbed into bed and went happily to sleep. But not one word of his experience did he share with his wife. That would wait until morning.

Since in this little house space was of the essence, Becky and Mary Ellen's beds occupied the same tiny sleeping loft as their parents'. In an attempt to gain some privacy, the Websters separated themselves from their children by draping a blanket over a taut cord. Mary Ellen, however, regarded this blanket as her own special way to wake up her sleeping parents. Each morning Don and Thelma awakened to Mary Ellen's cooing and laughing as she pulled the blanket back and forth in a game of peekaboo.

After Mary Ellen awakened him the next morning, Don immediately scrambled out of bed to examine his daughter's eye. It was just the same as the night before—crossed! Instantly a wave of doubt filled Don's mind. "I can't believe it isn't healed," he said to himself. And then Don experienced the same sense of buoyancy and expectancy as he had the night before.

Gathering Mary Ellen up in his arms, he went downstairs and sat her in the high chair. After stoking the fires, he turned to Mary Ellen and covered up her good eye. "Can you see Daddy?" he said gently. Mary Ellen's response was to sit quietly and not try to push his hand away.

Later, Thelma came down with Becky, but Don, still feeling a little strange about all that was happening, didn't tell Thelma, who as a nurse took a more pragmatic approach to such things. Finally after breakfast, he confided in his wife, and together they put the glasses with the patch on Mary Ellen. She didn't fight it. And during a midmorning visit by Cecilia Piper, Don had Mary Ellen walk to her, still with the patch on the good eye, and Mary Ellen walked directly to her.

When Don shared some of his previous night's

experience, Cecilia slapped him on the back and said, "What did you expect? God is still in the business of healing!" And so with their faith strengthened and believing that God was effecting a healing in Mary Ellen's eye, the Websters waited out the months while the TB medication did its work and they would once again return to Anchorage.

As the weeks passed and more and more people learned about Mary Ellen's condition, the Websters began experiencing various kinds of social pressure. Friends in Canada wrote, along with the Websters' parents, and urged them to bring Mary Ellen back "home" to Canada for the operation. Other well-meaning friends wrote Turner Blount, the Websters' director, who in turn wrote the Websters and urged them to have the operation as quickly as possible. Few of those who wrote knew all the circumstances, and Don wished he could have explained what had happened that Monday night and how much he wanted to trust God to heal.

But in the end, social pressure prevailed. On June 19, after a long tiring flight from Barrow, the Websters arrived in Anchorage, and Mary Ellen began the first of several preoperation examinations. With a few deft lines in his diary, Don began a kind of medical countdown of the events immediately prior to the operation.

June 19: The neurosurgeon says the eye appears improved. M.E.'s head grown over two cm. since last examination. Yet doctor not happy. M.E. has no leg reflex and he thinks something's wrong with central nervous system.

June 23: Medical report not encouraging. More brain pressure. Operation scheduled for Monday next.

June 24: M.E.'s ear o.k. but brain pressure continues. Discouraged. I wish I could fast till the operation. I seem to have lost contact with God.

June 26: Strong feeling of doom, i.e., operation. Have urge to postpone it.

June 28: [the day of the operation] "Except a corn of wheat die . . ." Will M.E. die? I guess we must die to self and let her have the operation. Yesterday poor girl broken up over blood tests, but left her when she was quite happy. Not crying.

The doctor was still dressed in his green surgical gown. His gauze face mask hung down under his chin and he was smiling.

"Mr. and Mrs. Webster, I've come to tell you the operation has gone well. You can see your daughter in the recovery room shortly. In the meantime, why don't you refresh yourself in the hospital cafeteria. By the time you're finished, your daughter will be coming out of the anesthesia. I'll call you. It shouldn't be too long."

But it was long. Longer than it should have been. Thelma was particularly worried. From her own nursing experience, she knew such delays could only mean one thing—complications! Finally, after what seemed an eternity, a flat voice on the hospital intercom summoned Don and Thelma to the waiting room. When they arrived, the same doctor greeted them. He wore the same green surgical gown, only this time he wasn't smiling.

"I regret to have to tell you this, but things aren't going well. We're not sure your daughter will live."

"Not sure your daughter will live." Don and Thelma heard them as words but they were just words, words that seemed to come from another dimension. Almost hollow words that didn't belong or have meaning for them, except that they suddenly felt cold.

The doctor continued, "Do you need a priest?"

"Thank you, no," said Thelma. "My husband is

an ordained minister, but we would like to use the chapel to pray."

Unknown to the Websters, Mary Ellen was at that moment on an artificial respirator. After the operation, when she was taken into the recovery room and turned over, her breathing mechanism suddenly stopped. Try as they might, the doctors were unable to induce her to breathe on her own. Even as the Websters prayed in the chapel, the respirator was pumping life-giving air to Mary Ellen's lungs, but her little heart was becoming weaker, and weaker, and weaker.

In the middle of all this, while they were in the chapel, Don felt an urge to pray over his daughter. At first the hospital administration declined his request. Then when they learned Don was a minister, they allowed him into the recovery room.

So there in front of three or four doctors and assorted medical staff, Don prayed. It was a simple prayer. It had to be. The pain of seeing his daughter's life slowly ebb away numbed his consciousness. But with courage and faith born of the confidence that God, if He so chose, could give his daughter strength to live, he asked for her life. But God the Creator, the giver of life, answered: *Death is not the end of life; it is the beginning. Be assured that this slight, momentary affliction is preparing for you an eternal weight of glory beyond all comparison . . . For the things that are seen are transient, but the things that are unseen are eternal.*

Mary Ellen's heart stopped. She was two years and one month.

Don and Thelma gave permission for a postmortem examination.★ Then while Don arranged for the body to be flown back to Wainwright for burial, Thel-

---

★The autopsy revealed that during the operation a tiny blood clot had lodged in the breathing center of Mary Ellen's brain.

ma walked out of the hospital and moved unthinkingly toward their borrowed car. She paused for a moment when she reached for the door handle and looked up. There was a sharp, clear, beautiful blue sky, and for that moment she felt utterly alone. There was no one there to share her grief and the pain that cut into her being stung as sharply as the cold on her naked face. In her grief and anger and frustration, still looking up into the sky, she said to herself, "It's a myth. There's no one out there. It's all a myth, there isn't any God. He doesn't exist. I've been fed a pack of lies. There is no one up there."

Exhausted, Thelma opened the car door and sank into the seat and wept. As she did, she was suddenly aware of the dual feelings racing through her. One was in her head and had given vent to her thoughts of disillusionment. The other came from her heart and seemed to say, *Have confidence, child, I'm still here.*

The inability to grieve is the inability to truly love and take solace and delight in human fellowship. In the months the Websters lived in Wainwright, the people had come to love and enjoy the energetic and dedicated *taaniks* (outsiders or white people) as one of their own. In fact, Mary Ellen had been given her own special Inupiat name—*Nanauk*. Therefore, when the plane arrived bearing her remains in a little coffin, the whole village was filled with sorrow. On July Fourth, Roy wrote a letter to the Websters who had stayed in Fairbanks for a few days' rest before returning to Wainwright for the burial.

Dear Don and Thelma:
First let me quote Job 1:21b: "The Lord gave and the Lord hath taken away, BLESSED BE THE NAME OF THE LORD." Yes, the strong in the faith can only say,

"Blessed be the name of the Lord." I know this is what you have done.

As soon as I found out about the loss (our loss, God's gain) of Mary Ellen, I asked John Chambers to come down and help with the funeral service. [He was the Presbyterian minister in Barrow.] The way I found out about the death of Mary Ellen was somewhat of a surprise. I happened to get out of the house and walk toward the bank just as Peter and Homer landed the skiff opposite our place. I watched them start unloading the mail from the skiff, and then the two of them started to carry what looked like a coffin, and I walked to meet them.

I could not think who this could be; I never thought of Mary Ellen. When I asked who it was, even before they were hardly close enough, they told me it was your daughter. It was a great shock to me. I groaned, and there were tears, and I grieved, but I took it in faith believing that she is in better hands than any of us can give her in this world.

It was the day before, Sunday, at our evening service that I called on the people to pray for you and the family as we have been doing. What you said in your letter, "The Lord never makes a mistake," is true indeed.

I received your letter after we stored the remains in our cellar. There will be no rush for you to come down. It will keep as long as you wish to remain in Barrow. Today is the 4th of July and after the celebration I will ask the men to set a time at their convenience for digging the grave. It should be complete before the funeral takes place.

Please continue to remember the words of God in the Bible as your personal comfort. I know you have them written in your heart and soul. The Lord be gracious unto you.

In Christian sympathy and love,
Roy (Signed).

Twenty-two days later, on July 26, the Websters wrote an open letter to all their friends about what had happened.

Wainwright, Alaska
July 26, 1961

"Except a corn of wheat fall into the ground and die it abideth alone, but if it die, it bringeth forth much fruit" (John 12:24). What a verse to read during morning devotions on the day we were to admit Mary Ellen to the hospital! In our minds we set aside the most obvious application for another, but thirty hours later, the first application that had suggested itself had become a reality and our little girl was in heaven.

We expected the Lord to heal her for life here on earth. He chose to heal her completely by removing her from the realm of sickness, sorrow and hardship. Living faith must be positive and expectant if it is to be effective, but at the same time we must allow for God's sovereignty. We have a beautiful picture of this in Daniel, chapter three, where the three young Hebrew men are arraigned before the indignant king for failing to bow before his image.

In giving defense they said, "If it be so, our God is able to deliver, and He will. But if not, we will not serve thy gods." They had confidence of deliverance, but still allowed for God's sovereignty. We have attempted to maintain this same balance in praying for Mary Ellen.

It was a lengthy letter and the Websters talked about how the crisis had drawn them closer to each other and to their Lord. There were also words about rededicating their lives to completing the work of translating the Scriptures for the Inupiat.

Then, in keeping with the Websters' unique sense of frugality and practicality, they asked that in the place of flowers those who felt led could contribute to the Mary Ellen Memorial Fund:

This fund will be used to erect a small cabin at our Fairbanks center. It will be used primarily as a place for our Wycliffe workers to stay in when they come from the outlying areas. There has been a need for this kind of cabin on our center. We know this tangible assistance to Bible translation will be a much appreciated memorial. We are looking to the Lord to supply the funds.

The letter continued strong, forward-looking, positive, with no hint of the inner pain the two parents had suffered. Neither were there many hints of how the people in the village had ministered and helped ease the pain.

Interestingly, one of those who ministered greatly to Don was the Pentecostal evangelist, M. M. Butterfield. It was this man's sensitive gift of encouragement that helped Don in his moments of grief and adjustment.

For Thelma, it was the women of the village who came in great numbers to sit and share with her their own losses. Perhaps for the first time they sensed Thelma's vulnerability and told her how they had wept over the children who had died from chicken pox, whooping cough, and other communicable diseases. "Once we buried sixteen children in a mass grave," said a woman. Then she named a neighbor who had lost three children at once.

Many of the people who visited came just to sit. They understood how to give the gift of their presence. Occasionally the gift was a little more demonstrative. The parents of Rosey (the little girl that Thelma had desperately tried to save from the effects of pneumonia) came. The man didn't say much. He didn't need to. He simply gave Thelma a hug. All this helped to relieve the tension and allowed the Websters to move back into their regular routine.

As tragic as all this was, Mary Ellen's death and her burial among the Inupiat dead amazed the villagers. Many had expected the Websters to leave. But when they returned and had the funeral and allowed the people to help and minister, a bond as deep as blood ties linked Don and Thelma forever to the people of Wainwright Village. In turn, this new relationship allowed for a greater expansion of their ministry among the Inupiat.

This didn't happen overnight. For some reason Thelma made a more rapid adjustment to the loss than did Don. It may have been because Thelma better understood the implications of coping with a child of limited competency, particularly in an isolated situation. The autopsy also revealed signs that Mary Ellen would be epileptic, and this with the other complications helped Thelma to conclude that God had been merciful in taking her daughter. Yet the wound of losing Mary Ellen still ached. Then one day while Thelma stood beside the gravesite thinking and remembering, a loud clear voice inside her said, *"She is not here. She is risen!"*

In that moment, Thelma realized God had blessed her with the joy of having her child for two full years, and in a prayer of thankfulness to God for the hope of the resurrection, the wound began to heal. What was left in her memory suddenly became more important than what had been lost. She was now free to continue on with the business of life in the sure confidence that one day both would see each other again.

For Don, the wound didn't (or he wouldn't allow it to) heal as rapidly as it had for Thelma. Part of the reason had to do with his continuing struggle with his doctrinal beliefs. During the revival he admitted God could indeed work in ways outside his preconceived ideas of "correct" and "incorrect" methods of worship. God, he discovered, could manifest himself through formal as well as informal channels, providing those who came to Him did so in spirit and in truth. But all this didn't help. Inside he was disappointed and disillusioned. He had been so sure God was going to answer his prayers for Mary Ellen. How could he deny that night when he knelt beside his bed and felt God nearer than his own body? He would never forget how clearly God had spoken to him about praying for his daughter's eye, and in some ways he felt there had been a healing going on. Why then, after all that, had God let her die? There were no answers. Silently he screamed for them.

In his enthusiasm for God and His Word, Don wanted to be ready to give an answer for the reality of his faith. His faith was living, vital, and he desired to speak to others with strength and certainty about this most important of all life's issues. This had been at the heart of his call to serve with Wycliffe. Yet this desire for answers seemed to be working against him because the answers he wanted had to pass through his own rationale. Ever since seminary it had been difficult for him to accept doctrines that didn't square with his own understanding of biblical interpretation. Admittedly he had reexamined his thinking about the Holy Spirit during the revival, but when events didn't work out according to his presuppositions, he again began to probe and ponder the Scriptures.

As he did, a new outlook about life, about himself, and about his theology slowly began to emerge into his understanding. First, he admitted to himself he was indulging in a little bit of self-pity. Second, and hinged on the first, was a new understanding of the work of the Holy Spirit. Before, most of his understanding had been theory. Oh, he was aware of the Spirit's leading, but the pain of his daughter's death unveiled a new dynamic to the Holy Spirit's function. From the promise Jesus gave to His disciples in John 14:16, Don learned anew that the Holy Spirit is the *Paraclete,* or Helper, the One who comes alongside, not just as a counselor, guide, advocate, teacher, and friend, but the One who in the midst of life's darkest moments gives the believer courage and power to cope with life. Out of his anguish and frustration came the realization that the Holy Spirit was just as much at work helping him during his suffering and adversity as when He displayed his outpouring power during a revival. In a way that went beyond his human reasoning, Don was to come to the place where he admitted his pain was a unique gift, because the same Holy Spirit who infused him with strength and courage to carry on gave him a new understanding of how he could serve and comfort others in similar circumstances of pain and frustration. The basis for this understanding came from the Apostle Paul who in 2 Corinthians 1:3–7 said:

What a wonderful God we have—he is the Father of our Lord Jesus Christ, the source of every mercy, and the one who so wonderfully comforts and strengthens us in our hardships and trials. And why does he do this? So that when others are troubled, needing our sympathy and encouragement, we can pass on to them this same help and comfort God has given to us. You can be sure that the more we undergo sufferings for Christ, the more he will shower us with his comfort and encouragement *(Living Bible)*.

The truth of these words were words of promise. They were not fulfilled immediately for the Websters, but gradually, as people came and found in Don and Thelma an empathetic and authentic understanding, particularly when a person expressed a lack of confidence in God. Perhaps one reason why people came to appreciate Don's ability as a counselor was his reluctance to try and defend God. Rather, he encouraged the grieving person to tell God exactly how he felt. Don's prototype was Job, who in Job 13:10 said: "Anyone who uses lies to try and help God out is in serious trouble" *(LB)*. Taking a further cue from the last part of verse 15 of that same chapter, Don suggested that when they had a grievance against God, to do as Job did and "argue their case with him." In doing this, it was Don's hope that such a person would come to understand that they could learn as he had learned: when one comes face to face with the personhood of God, he can live without answers and let God be God. This suggested to Don's mind that he could no longer give quick, easy, or superficial answers to the problem of tragic pain. He resolved to bypass any attempt at trying to reconcile the paradox of good and evil. His comments had more to do with reminding people that God knows about our personal agony and that He grieves just as we grieve. He suggested that one of the best ways to come to terms with life's paradoxes was to celebrate one's dependence upon God by accepting these paradoxes. Christians are called to live their lives by faith, meaning, we live our lives without demanding answers to our questions. It should be enough that God knows the end from the beginning and ultimately has our best interests at heart.

While the Websters truly desired to live by these concepts, it would not entirely free them from further anxiety. Within twelve months, Thelma would twice experience some temporary discouragement and know the same cold jagged fears and sense of helplessness as she had on the day Mary Ellen died. And the first was to come just one month after she and Don had laid Mary Ellen in the permafrost grave.

11

You Should Have Heard the Hallelujahs

A hunter coming in off the ice spotted them, and with a single, *"Agvik"* (bowhead), sent a bolt of electricity through the hunting crews and community of Wainwright. Nothing in the Arctic dominates an Inupiat's coming and going, nor occupies his attention, nor saps his strength so completely and compellingly and with so much excitement as does the whale hunt. With that one word, the hopes of ice cellars filled with delicious *muktuk*—that thick crunchy outer skin of the whale—propelled everyone into action, including Don.

Don's crew chief checked over his shoulder gun, a vintage model that shot a black powder bomb with a fuse set to explode five seconds after penetrating the whale. Others of the crew (there were five other men, including Don), readied the *umiak*. Long sealskin lines, harpoons, and inflated sealskin floats were placed in the bottom of the *umiak* with the same care and precision of a conductor arranging members of his orchestra. And the *umiak* itself was outfitted with a small, flat-bottom wooden sled to pull it over the ice toward the open lead.

Every year since his arrival in Wainwright, Don had spent a week each season camped out on the ice hunting for whale. To be sure, shooting a fifty- to sixty-ton animal while bobbing up and down in a fifteen- to twenty-foot walrus skin boat that the mighty bowhead could crush as easily as an eggshell has to be the height of madness and unequaled spine-tingling excitement. The first time Don saw the great leviathan surface and begin with its cavernous mouth to scoop in tons of frigid water to feed on the shrimplike crustaceans that lie near the surface of the water, he was struck dumb by its immense size. "It was as if an island had suddenly appeared in front of our little boat," said Don.

There were many important reasons for Don to accompany the Inupiat men on their hunts. There was no finer way to hear the language spoken with all its natural flow and interesting idioms. And this is precisely what a translator must be sensitive to if he is to produce a translation that the people will recognize as their own.

From an anthropological point of view, participating with the people in their natural environment allows the translator to observe the complex and subtle rules of the culture. Knowing and understanding the relationship of common knowledge, laws, beliefs, and customs of a given people (knowing how and where to place the whale hunting gear in the *umiak* is common knowledge), allows a translator to produce a powerful idiomatic translation.*

From the very beginning, Don had shown his eagerness to understand and accept the Inupiat's in-

---

*For further information on the importance and relationship of culture and language to Bible translation, see Hugh Steven's book, *The Man With The Noisy Heart,* published by Moody Press.

teresting cultural insights. Above all, Don wanted to be treated not as a *taanik* (outsider) but as one with his Inupiat friends. But in their characteristic noncommital way, his Eskimo friends said not a word about how they felt having him along on the hunt. And that day, as everyone worked together as a well practiced team, yet with no one giving commands, Don thought about the first time he went out hunting on the ice, and how much he had learned.

It was early spring of 1959. This time the hunting crew and Don were after walrus. In many ways, going out after walrus is more dangerous than hunting bowhead. While the bowhead has infinitely more strength than the walrus, it is less ferocious when attacked. As one Arctic writer once wrote, "Hunting the walrus in the dark from a thin and flexible platform of ice at the very edge of a 'smoking' sea is one of the greatest tests of courage."

A herd animal, the walrus with amazing strength and speed (in the water), can become a ton of heaving fearless fury bent on destroying any and all intruders. Don was quite unaware of all this that spring, and perhaps it was just as well the crew didn't encounter the walrus on that trip. A year later on another walrus hunt when Don was more seasoned, they did bag a walrus and one of the men offered Don first choice of the blood-soaked and still twitching walrus brains. Don chuckled to himself as he remembered that incident, and recalled stories of other translators in other places eating strange things out of courtesy to their hosts. He had always thought he would be able to rise to such an occasion, but when he had looked at those brains, he could only smile, shake his head and say, "After you." And then he remembered how, with the same sense of joy and relief a host might express when the last piece of tasty chicken is declined by a guest and he gets to have it after all, the hunter smiled and began at once to devour the delicacy.

Don's reverie was interrupted with the selection of a campsite on the ice, next to an open lead. The first item out of the *umiak* was their tent—a large square of white tarpaulin. As Don set the tent poles and secured the sealskin guy lines with tent pegs driven into the sea ice, he remembered again what it was like back in 1959 when he first set up such a camp.

With the exception of Don, everyone knew exactly what to do. The other Inupiat men had lost count of the number of times they had set up a hunting camp on the ice. For them it was as natural and automatic as an Idaho farmer planting potatoes. Aware he was a neophyte, Don held back a few paces and watched what the other men did, then followed suit. After the tent was up, one of the men unloaded a cut-down oil drum from the *umiak*. It was June, but in the Arctic, out on the ice, the men needed this blubber-burning stove to ward off the sub-zero chill factor from the raw wind that pulled at their tent flap.

After the cut-down oil drum stove was set in place with several lengths of pipe protruding through the canvas roof to carry away the belching black smoke from the whale blubber that had been stuffed inside, Don helped the men carry in the deerskin sleeping bags. Before the sleeping bags were laid down, however, one of the men spread out a layer of caribou skin as insulation from the ice floor. Next out of the *umiak* was the all-important hunting box. No crew ever forgot this necessary item, for this box contained pots and pans, a kettle, and a Primus stove to boil their meat and water for their all important tea. The hunting box also contained tools and extra shells for the rifles.

While one man set about to boil water for tea, another clambered up an ice hummock, and with an old telescope began to scan the seascape and broken ice in search of animal life, particularly walrus. It would be this man's responsibility to look for animals and to warn the others, who might be sleeping, of any unusual shifting of wind or current, or of sudden ice breakup.

With the camp's readiness, the men's expectations began to mount. The ice cellars in Wainwright were becoming empty, and there were people and dogs to feed. Although he didn't quite know what to expect, Don also began to feel that same contagion of expectancy, and about an hour after the camp was set up, the man with the telescope called out to the others. As he pointed out to sea, the word was not *"Agvik"* (walrus), but *"Ugruk"* (bearded seal).

Within seconds the hunters raced to launch the *umiak*. Every moment was calculated to return the best and most efficient and practical use of energy and time. To make sure not a moment would be lost launching the *umiak,* the stern rested on a small piece of ice, thus pitching it at a slight angle with the bow facing the open lead. This was done so that with the first signs of activity in the water, the men, on the run and never missing a stride, could grab opposite sides of the gunwales, race toward the water, gently bounce into the boat, and begin to paddle with quick, even strokes through the ice slush sea toward the quarry.

And that's exactly the way it happened. The only difference was that no one had told Don how it was done, and he was almost left behind. When the *umiak* came to about fifty feet of the seal's dark head bobbing up and down in the cold black water, the men stopped paddling and sat absolutely still. The one exception was the one man who slowly picked up his rifle while never once taking his eyes off the seal's gray-black head. Feeding a shell into the breach, he deftly brought the rifle to his shoulder and took aim.

He was about to squeeze the trigger when the seal suddenly slipped out of sight. The man lowered his rifle but kept his unbroken gaze on the sea in front of the *umiak*. No one spoke. Don felt the tension mounting like the silence before a thunderbolt. After what seemed to be longer than the usual two to three minutes seals stay submerged, it reappeared. This time it surfaced about thirty feet off the *umiak's* stern.

Again the hunter brought the rifle to his shoulder and carefully tried to catch the bobbing head in his sights. For just an instant, Don saw the seal stop his sea dance, and in that instant, a sharp crack broke the polar silence, and the seal rolled over and floated high in the water. The harvest had begun. It would take many more seals and hopefully a walrus to satisfy the hunger demands of the Inupiat of Wainwright Village, but the men accepted this first seal as a hopeful sign of more to come.

Pleased with their effort and thankful to God for His supply, the men returned to their ice camp and immediately set about to feast on their good fortune. In the customary manner, a man opened up the seal's breast and cut out a chunk of rib meat and blubber and dumped them into a pot to boil.

Entering into the flow and rhythm of camp life, Don noticed how each man with his hunting knife (his only utensil) cut off a chunk of meat from out of the pot. This chunk was held between the teeth and with a swish of the hunting knife, cut off in front of the face leaving a thin sliver of meat dangling out of the mouth. Next a cube of blubber was cut and placed in the teeth. At that moment the two morsels were devoured together.

It took a little practice, but Don was soon cutting

and snipping blubber and seal meat like a pro. The only problem he had was with the blubber. Occasionally the blubber, which is really loose oil in membrane formation, dribbled down on his parka. When that happened to the other men, they used the back of their hands to wipe it up, then slurped it off, and Don did the same.

At the time Don was snipping and slurping, not a man made a single comment. It was as if Don had been doing this all his life. But years later at a farewell party for the Websters when they moved to Fairbanks, some of the men sat around telling stories about all the strange and funny experiences the Websters had had. And one of the men said, "That *Webstarak,* he may have gotten lost and done some strange things, but I know when he really became our friend. It was that time we went out walrus hunting and got an *ugruk* instead, and he ate the meat and blubber together. That time he showed he didn't think he was better than us. That was the time he became a true Eskimo!"

Don enjoyed being with the men. In spite of his limited understanding of the language and Eskimo ways and the crew's limited comprehension of English, there was an intimate camaraderie even when there were long periods of silence. On one occasion a friend asked Don how he handled the long silences. He responded with, "There is something in Inupiat culture that lends itself to wholesome silence. In our Western culture it seems we have filled the air with sound. Not so among the Inupiat. They are cozy and comfortable to sit for a long time without saying a word. In fact, one of the most secure, comfortable feelings I have known was, after a hard day of hunting in the cold, to lie relaxed in my sleeping bag, feeling toasty warm, waiting for the meat to boil. Everyone was content to just be by himself. We didn't have to talk. We were content knowing that we had all shared a hard day on the ice."

Satisfied after their meal of seal meat and blubber, the men sat quietly working until another animal was sighted. Suddenly, without warning, a fierce wind erupted sending heavy breakers crashing onto the ice. Then slowly, ponderously at first, the ice began to move. The currents, much to Don's dismay, were doing to his ice floe exactly what they had done to Roy Ahmaogak so many years before—pushing them out to sea.

Don eyed the men and received some minor consolation from the casual way they broke camp and repacked the *umiak*. "The storm will have to get worse before it gets better," said one of the men. "We will head for shore and wait it out." Expertly the men lashed the *umiak* to the small wooden sled and headed across the ice away from the fury of the storm.

Under the warmer June sun, the ice had become rotten and honeycombed with holes and cracks. In order for the men to reach shore, they had to tow the *umiak* by sealskin lines tied to the gunwales and struggle up and over huge pans of ice that were constantly in motion, slamming and creaking together with unimaginable groanings. Frequently they came to large puddles of bone-chilling water that had to be forded. If they could, the men floated the *umiak* across, but sometimes there was no choice but to wade through. To avoid falling through these cold black holes, the hunters probed in the meltwater with long sticks. Don quickly learned to pay special attention to those foreboding black puddles that meant only one thing if the probe went straight down—it was open all the way down to the ocean beneath!

Once away from the fierce edge of the open lead, the men relaxed a bit and made their way toward the safety of the shore. Once they made landfall, they again set up camp. Since they couldn't return to Wainwright by sea, and since the wind and current had carried them more than fifty miles from home, they had no alternative but to sit and wait out the storm. Unhappily for Don, it turned out to be a long five days of eating nothing but *ugruk* meat and blubber.

Thelma wasn't too worried. She knew her husband was in good, experienced hands, but she did heave a sigh of relief when on the afternoon of the sixth day some children spotted the *umiak* struggling to get through the ice-choked bay opposite the village. Though they were less than a mile from the village, it took Don and the men over two hours to push aside the huge pans of ice and work their way through to shore. In some ways, these last two hours were Don's most difficult of the entire ordeal.

After six days in the warm sun, the stench of the rotting *ugruk* (the men had taken a total of three) made it hard for Don to keep his stomach in place. At one point, just as they were about to reach shore, several long worms wriggled out of the half-open mouth of one of the dead *ugruk*. The stench, the worms, and having to sit on top of the rotting carcasses while he paddled, was almost more than his system could handle. Just as he was about to retch, the bow of the *umiak* bumped the black gravel beach, and Don jumped out to safety.

As a harvesting trip, it was only mildly successful. But as a trip to firmly convince the people of the village that Don was more than a *taanik,* the trip was a huge success. Don's willingness to endure the hardships of the hunt and to eat the same food as his Inupiat companions without complaining showed everyone that here indeed was a man who could be trusted. And if the man could be trusted and respected, then the words he spoke about God could also be trusted. Those five-plus days with the hunting crew became a great investment for the cause of the Inupiat New Testament, because among the Inupiat, it is always more important from *whom* one learns, than *what* one learns. Don had shared intimately in the common struggle for the preservation of life itself, and the Inupiat loved him for it.

That had all happened in 1959, three years earlier. Since that time Don had accompanied the men on many hunting expeditions and all had proceeded without serious incident. And at the beginning of this hunting trip in June 1962, it looked as if this one might be one of those to catalog in the halls of one's idyllic memory. But Don was to remember this trip for an event that quite eclipsed his first hunting experience out on the ice.

The Inupiat are people who respond more to events than the clock, and since this was that time of year when the sun circled high in the horizon for twenty-four hours of sunlight, there were no definitive times to sleep. Normally, when there was game to harvest, they hunted for as long as it was possible, taking time out to catnap whenever there was a lull in the hunting or fishing. On this particular day, the men were tired after traveling and setting up camp, and except for the one who stood guard, they all flopped into their sleeping bags, fully clothed, even to the wearing of their *mukluks* (boots). One never knew when the ice might break or a whale would be sighted. If that happened, no one wanted to waste precious seconds getting dressed. But Don, contrary to custom, took off his *mukluks* before going to sleep.

In many cultures, people are warned of impending doom by the clang of a bell, the erratic screeching of a siren, or the high pitched buzz of a smoke alarm. In Inupiat culture, you are awakened by someone's fingers quickly flicking the soles of your boots. When that happens on an ice camp, no one says a word. They immediately leap up and dash for the safety of the *umiak*, because such a signal can only mean imminent danger from ice breakup.

And about 4:00 A.M. when Don was awakened by a flick on his feet, he knew they were in for big trouble. The ice was shivering and heaving and buckling like a gigantic water bed. "It's a back swell," said one man, and everyone leapt to their feet.

Unknown to the sleeping men, the guard had fallen asleep and hadn't sensed the signs of a storm brewing out at sea. By the time he was aware, huge waves had backed up under the ice, and it was almost too late to warn the rest of the men.

As it was, by the time Don got into his boots, the section of ice where he and the rest of the men had camped had, with a great grinding and cracking, broken off from the main landlocked ice. To their dismay, they found themselves on an ice floe smaller than a single story cottage—about twenty by thirty feet—and they were floating out into the heavy seas.

Frantically, the men scrambled to gather up whatever was closest to them—guns first, sleeping bags, pots and pans, stove, the three sets of stovepipes, the furs they had laid down for insulation. All these they dumped haphazardly into the *umiak* as the ice block was moving farther and farther into the sea that was becoming choppier and choppier. Suddenly an ominous crack appeared and split off a third of the ice block, separating the men from their tent that was still erected. Without a second thought, Don jumped over the crack, pulled out the stakes, collapsed the tent and jumped back before the crack widened. Hurriedly the men dumped the large square of canvas into the *umiak,* grabbed the gunwales, and flung the boat into the water.

Normally, the launching of an *umiak* by a group of seasoned hunters goes as smoothly as a well-rehearsed drill team. But not on this day. As the men set the boat into the water and scrambled to get themselves inside, the boat, lopsided with the hurriedly placed equipment, suddenly tipped sideways. Pots, pans, stove, stovepipes and other valuable hard-to-replace pieces of equipment spilled and sank into the turbulent sea. Fortunately the rifles, usually placed on top of the equipment for quick access, were in the bottom of the *umiak* along with the whaling equipment.

Stoically the men accepted their losses and headed back to the shore. When they had paddled to within three to four hundred yards of the shore, Don turned to see their ice island split into yet another third. Once ashore, the men climbed a small ice hummock and watched in silence as the heavy seas further reduced their ice island to chunks the size of compact cars. Inwardly Don thanked the Lord for getting them all off with no more than a few lost articles.

With most of their equipment lost, the men returned immediately to Wainwright arriving around noon. And like the first trip, Thelma rushed out to greet her husband. The only difference this time was that Thelma almost broke down in tears when she saw her husband trudging up the beach.

Later, when Don shared with Thelma his harrowing experience with the ice breaking up around him, he learned the reason for Thelma's emotional greeting.

"I can't explain why," Thelma said, "but about 3:30 this morning I woke up with a start and a terrible foreboding about your safety. I knew you were with an experienced crew, but still felt I should pray for your safety. So I obeyed the nudging and kept a prayer vigil until about 5:00 A.M."

"What made you stop then?" asked Don.

"I don't really know, except that it was just around five that the anxiety for your safety left me, and I went back to bed and slept with a sense of peace."

"That's most interesting, indeed," said Don, "because it was just about 5:00 A.M. when we reached the shore!"

Serious students of Scripture agree that the goal of a true Christian is the formation of a character conformed to the image of Christ that may one day be presented without shame to God. After our initial acceptance of God's salvation through faith in His Son Jesus, God begins to conform us, step by step, into a life of faith, obedience, and trust. We begin to realize our "momentary troubles are achieving us an eternal glory that far outweighs them all" (2 Cor. 4:17), and that these problems are necessary for spiritual traction and a life of daily dependence upon God.

Thelma and Don never outwardly, or even inwardly, admitted they had the slightest hesitancy in trusting God for whatever He brought into their lives. The obvious evidence of their personal faith and trust in God's sovereignty was plain for all to see. Yet God, who knows the heart better than the individual himself, used an incident in Thelma's life (Don's too, but more directly in Thelma's) to show that her confidence in God wasn't as it once had been.

The incident occurred about three months after the birth of Don and Thelma's third daughter, Julie Ann, born April 4, 1962 and weighing in at seven pounds, two ounces. Like her older sister Becky, Julie Ann was in every way a perfectly normal child. On this day, two-year-old Becky bounced over to where Thelma was feeding her new little sister and accidentally gave Julie Ann a hard pushing jolt.

Almost before Thelma could caution Becky to be more careful, Julie Ann regurgitated her milk and began to cry. It was a cry unlike anything Thelma had heard before, high-pitched and quite abnormal. At first Thelma suspected Julie Ann might have a broken rib. Along with refusing to eat, there was a haunting look of deep anxiety in her face, and she couldn't seem to breathe properly.

For several days Thelma monitored her three-month-old daughter, but couldn't determine exactly what the problem could be. When a week passed and there was still no sign of improvement, Thelma caught the weekly mail flight and flew to Barrow. Unknown to Thelma, the pilot radioed ahead and arranged for Dr. Jones, the only doctor to service the several thousand people of Barrow and the surrounding area, to meet the plane. It took just one look from Dr. Jones to make his diagnosis.

"She's really in a bad way," he said cautiously. "It looks like it could be congestive heart failure, but I'm not sure what's causing it."

As the doctor spoke, Thelma felt her knees weaken and a sudden jolt hit her stomach. Her mind flashed back to Mary Ellen and in desperation she cried out to the Lord. "O Lord, not again. Please, not again! Not another doctor to recite a list of things wrong with my baby. Lord, Lord, what are you doing to us? What are you doing?"

"Mrs. Webster? Mrs. Webster? Did you hear what I was just saying?"

"I'm sorry," said Thelma. "I was thinking. You . . . you said you didn't know . . ."

"Yes, I'm sorry. I don't know the best way to treat your daughter. However, I'll be putting her in an incubator. I have a pediatrician friend in Anchorage whom I'll phone immediately. In the meantime, why don't you try to get some rest."

Later that afternoon, Thelma returned to the hospital and found that the doctor, in consultation with his colleague in Anchorage, had determined Julie Ann's

condition as paroxysmal tachycardia with auricular fib-
rillation. It was this that caused the congestive heart
failure. "The medicine we've prescribed hasn't as yet
had any immediate effect on your daughter's condition," said Dr. Jones. "It's just going to take a bit of
time. Actually, it's a miracle she has lived as long as she
has. Her liver is enlarged into her lower abdomen and
her feet are severely swollen."

From the hospital back to the Presbyterian manse
where Thelma was staying was only half a block. But as
she trudged along that cold, windswept, crunchy gravel
road, she felt as if she were in a bad dream walking mile
after endless mile. With tears welling up inside ready to
explode, hot insupportable tears that wouldn't spill out,
she painfully reminisced. "Here it is just a year after
Mary Ellen died, and now again I am losing another one
of my babies. O Lord, Lord, how can I cope?"

Just before she reached the manse, Thelma suddenly was impressed with the notion of going over to the
Assemblies of God church where they were having special revival meetings. She would ask them to pray for
Julie Ann. But just as quickly as she had the momentary
impression, she pushed it aside and went straight to the
manse.

Once inside, she again felt the nudge to go to the
special revival meeting. "No," she said to herself, "we
prayed for Mary Ellen and she died. I don't want to go
through all that again."

But the more she resisted, the stronger was the
impression that she should ask the people to pray. At
last, reluctantly, she slipped on her parka and walked
over to the church and told the pastor and his wife, Mr.
and Mrs. Bills, about Julie Ann's condition.

"I don't know what's going to happen," she said
dejectedly, "nor does the doctor. But would you please
ask the people to pray?"

The next morning Thelma returned to the hospital to an astounded doctor who said again, "It's a miracle that your daughter has lived for a week with such a congested heart. You can go in now and take her out of the oxygen tent and feed her."

To her utter amazement, Thelma was greeted by a happy smiling baby who showed not the slightest sign of being in any discomfort.

That afternoon, Don flew in from Wainwright with Becky, and Thelma had the hard job of explaining to him how serious the doctor considered Julie Ann's condition to be. "She seems to be improving," said Thelma, "but we still have to wait and see." And then she told Don how she had struggled with allowing herself to believe God would answer her prayers.

Still later that day while Don and Thelma sat with the Presbyterian pastor and his wife over a light supper, Dr. Jones came to see the Websters. From her past hospital experience, Thelma knew that when a busy doctor makes the effort to see a waiting family, you can expect the worst. And when the doctor asked if he might speak to the Websters alone, Thelma began to brace herself for the jolt.

"You know," said the doctor, "it's always the nurse who carries the good news to a waiting family and it's the doctor who carries the bad. But in your case I wanted to change the rules. I've come to tell you that your little daughter is all right. There is absolutely nothing wrong with her. The liver is back to normal size, the swelling has gone from her feet, and she doesn't need oxygen. Her heart and breathing are normal; you can take her home tonight."

The doctor then explained that neither he nor his colleague had ever seen congestive heart failure in one so young. "The nerves that control the heart somehow were 'knocked' out of control," said the doctor. "We can't guarantee it won't happen again, but otherwise she is perfectly normal. For someone who had congestive heart failure the evening before, it's nothing short of a miracle for her to be going home tonight. Yes indeed, nothing short of a miracle!"

Later Don and Thelma took their precious bundle back to the manse, and that night Don attended the Assembly of God's revival service and reported what the doctor had said a few hours earlier. When Don returned to the manse after the meeting, he relaxed on the bed next to Thelma and said simply, "Honey, when I told them what the doctor said about Julie Ann and that she came home tonight, you should have heard the hallelujahs!"

During the days that followed this difficult incident, Don and Thelma came to the conclusion that God wanted them to know He does answer prayers for healing. With Mary Ellen His answer had been to take her where she'd be completely well—forever; with Julie Ann it was for this time and space. Thelma also prayed that Julie Ann would have no permanent heart damage and as of this writing, she is a vivacious twenty-year-old college student in good health.

While the difficult experience with Julie Ann caused the Websters to relive the anguish of Mary Ellen, both gained new insights, by degrees, into God's grace in their lives. Grappling together and separately, they reached the conclusion that God had His reasons for taking Mary Ellen. Both accepted and rested in His decision and found comfort in the truth expressed by Isaiah, the prophet, who said:

The righteous perish, and no one ponders it in his heart; devout men are taken away, and no one understands that the righteous are taken away *to be spared from evil* (57:1, *New International Version,* italics mine).

Released now from this pressure, Don turned with vigor to the task that had brought him to Alaska—Bible translation. He and Roy had a deadline to meet, and time was running out.

12

He Being Dead Yet Speaketh

They should have been happy—even ecstatic. The long anticipated goal of completing the Inupiat New Testament within five years was a reality. But Don and Roy were anything but happy.

In January 1964, the Websters requested and received permission to spend three months at the recently constructed Wycliffe center in Fairbanks* in a special translation workshop. During that three-month period, Don checked the translation with a representative from the Bible Society and three other Wycliffe colleagues who had completed their own translations of Scripture into ethnic languages.

After they completed the three-month workshop, the Websters gave the Inupiat Gospel of John, Ephesians, James and 1 John to the printers to be printed in a single volume. Ordinarily, this would gladden the heart

---

*It was at this center that the Mary Ellen Memorial Cabin was constructed. Donations from fellow Wycliffites and interested friends had been overwhelming, and by January 1962 the cabin was ready for occupancy.

of any first term translator, but not Don. He was frustrated. The three months of concentrated translation checking served only to confirm the mounting evidence against the way he and Roy had done their translating. Just before they left with their two children in May 1964 to return to Canada for their first furlough, Don was seriously thinking of resigning from Wycliffe and scuttling his translation program.

The reason for this dramatic turn of events was that after five years of hard diligent work, the American Bible Society, who had assumed publishing responsibility for the Inupiat New Testament, ruled the translation, "too wooden, too literal, and the Inupiat words are too long to function in a practical orthography."

While Don didn't fully agree with the Bible Society's assessment that the Inupiat words were too long,★ he felt the issue was one of communication—how to carry across in the translation the meaning of the original New Testament writer. Intuitively, Don perceived the Inupiat New Testament should sound as if Peter and Paul and John and all the other New Testament writers were native-born Inupiat. In a word, he wanted to produce an Inupiat New Testament with all the sparkle and freshness of the contemporary Inupiatun language.

Don had worked long enough with the language to understand that word order, idioms, and metaphors are different in different languages. To merely substitute an English (or Greek) word for an Inupiat word would

★The Inupiatun language is known linguistically as an *agglutinative* language. That is, a speaker of this language "glues" together suffixes to make one long complex sentence, a process much like adding boxcars to a locomotive. Don's careful linguistic analysis, plus his further consultation with linguistic scholars, had concluded that "glued" together words to form long sentences in Inupiat could not be separated or made shorter without destroying the unity of the sentence.

never convey the true meaning of a particular Scripture passage. The stilted, often meaningless word for word substitution of his own interlinear Greek/English New Testament clearly showed him that rhythm and euphony in a translation are as important as the meaning of the words and phrases. Yet many of these important facets of Bible translation were absent in the first draft of their translation. Don knew he needed to make radical adjustments, and he also knew he would need help to do it.

Don, of course, wasn't the only one who felt the need of additional help. The Bible Society's decision not to publish the Inupiat New Testament in its present form hit Roy particularly hard. He, after all, had carried the burden for the Scriptures to be translated into his mother tongue for over half his life. And now this most important of works, the thing he had dreamed of ever since he made that first dog sled trip to Demarcation Point in the 1920s, was seemingly doomed to failure.

In their new-older car that Director Turner Blount had purchased for them that spring and driven to Fairbanks, the Websters drove to Vancouver to visit friends before going across Canada to Ontario for their first furlough. During their drive through British Columbia's beautiful Okanagan Valley, Don found himself thinking more about the translation problem than being enriched by the spectacular beauty of the valley's endless miles of fruit orchards and pristine lakes.

"What do we do?" asked Don rhetorically of Thelma. "Do we go back to Wainwright after furlough and repeat what we've already done only to have the Bible Society reject it again?"

For the moment it was an unanswerable question. And the little family drove on in silence, each with their own frustrations and discouragements. Except that Thelma, with her God-given womanly optimism, suggested things might look better when they could look at their problems from a distance.

The distance was to be not only in time, but in actual physical miles—about 5000 of them—from Wainwright to the heart of old Mexico. It was the outskirts of the Otomi Indian village of Ixmiquilpan, a hundred miles northeast of Mexico City, that became the setting for the salvation of the Inupiat New Testament.

Turner Blount, who himself had worked on the Navajo New Testament, was aware of and shared Don's frustration over what to do about making the Inupiat New Testament both accurate and meaningfully intelligible to Inupiat readers. After allowing the Websters time to be reunited with family and friends in Ontario, Turner wrote Don and suggested he and Roy attend the Summer Institute of Linguistics' recently constructed translation workshop site in Mexico.

"The workshop is run by John Beekman and a team of trained translation consultants," wrote Turner. "John has had wide translation experience with the Chol people in southern Mexico and in a new and stimulating way is sharing his experience and insight into how to produce dynamic idiomatic translations. Many of the older translators who have taken the three-month workshop report they wish they had had John's translation helps twenty years ago."

Don and Roy had no way of knowing exactly what kind of man this John Beekman was, nor of the help, if any, he could give them in one of his workshops. After all, the treatment at the hands of some of the other consultants had been terribly devastating. Would this John Beekman be different? Who indeed was this man?

After serving first as a Wycliffe translator and then as Wycliffe's chief translation coordinator, Dr. John Beekman, in the early 1960s, almost singlehandedly defined for the whole Wycliffe organization what Bible translation was all about. But as important as his scholarly and practical help was to the world of Wycliffe and the cause of Bible translation, it was John's personal Christian character and method of dealing sensitively and empathetically with each one who came to him for help and counsel that marked the uniqueness of his ministry. One translator wrote:

> I wish there was some way I could begin to tell you how marvelous it is for me to have such confidence in you. It is a comfort to know you can see what the problems are and how best to solve them and to know that if I bring you a stupid problem (which I have on occasion), you will never make me feel stupid. Thank you for always being so kind and considerate.*

Had Don and Roy actually known what kind of help they would have received and what new concepts of communication they would learn, they surely would have left immediately for Mexico. But Don couldn't leave immediately. He first had to work out a strategy and ask Roy if he would be willing to give another year of concentrated work on the New Testament. In his letter to Roy about this, he told him that this year of study would begin with a three-month study period in Mexico, and that if he could leave his beloved Arctic for these three or four months, it just might result in the translation being okayed for publication.

As it happened, Don's letter to Roy couldn't have been more perfectly timed. Roy, at age sixty-seven, had just retired from his pastoral duties in Wainwright. He agreed he would go with Don to Mexico and afterward

---

*John Beekman died August 10, 1980, but for a further account of his life, read Hugh Steven's book, *The Man With the Noisy Heart,* Moody Press, 1979.

work together at the translation center in Fairbanks for as long as it took to complete the translation.

True to his unique method of avoiding the temptation to deflate or in any way crush Don or Roy for their previous work on the translation, John Beekman first complimented the two men on what they had accomplished. He particularly praised the men on their timetable and schedule they worked out to reach their goal of translating the New Testament in five years. Thus Don and Roy began the daily lectures full of expectancy and feeling that perhaps there was some hope after all.

Each day the men began with a series of lectures by John on a variety of translation procedures. These included ways of translating the images and symbolism of the New Testament, such as wineskins, whitewashed sepulchers, and fox (in reference to Herod).

"The New Testament is laced with metaphors and similes," said John, "and since the New Testament writers used images out of their own culture, it follows that many of the metaphorical images in the New Testament carry no meaning, or often an incorrect meaning, when translated literally into another language and another culture.

"For example, in a number of languages spoken here in Mexico, the word *sheep* is used to mean more than the noun. One language uses the word *sheep* in reference to someone who doesn't understand. Speakers in another language use the word to mean someone with long hair. For yet another language, *sheep* means a drunkard who when hit, does not yell. In still another language, the people talk of one who hangs around waiting for girls or who follows girls as *sheep*. Therefore, when you translate such verses as John 1:29: 'Behold the Lamb of God which taketh away the sin of the world,' it is imperative that the people who read these words understand the *meaning* behind the word *lamb*. The meaning, of course, is that Jesus Christ was to become the ultimate sacrifice for human sin."

At this point in the lecture, John Beekman paused, and though he fought the often searing pain of severe angina and struggled with a body weakened by a defective aortic valve, his spirit and resolve were strong. Whenever he spoke of the importance of idiomatic translations, he seemed a mighty man of physical strength. "I believe the essential principle of translation is for the translator to convey meaning in the text. The object of the translator is to bring about an effect equivalent to that produced by the author upon the hearts and minds of the original readers. Further, it can't be too fully stressed that the original authors wrote in a form that was natural and idiomatic at the time of their writing."★

As Don listened, he began to feel as if at last a great light of translation understanding had suddenly broken in upon him. Not so for Roy. To his own amazement, he found he held to a more literal position. In his interpretive method of translating, Roy had relied on the *form* of the text, followed by his own commentary. Now here he was being challenged to think more about the *content* or meaning of the text. In a way, Roy had assumed that all languages were basically the same; that he could move easily from a source language to a receptor language and translate the nouns and verbs in a one-to-one equivalent.

It took Roy about two weeks to come to the place Don was after the first couple of days at the workshop. One reason he was finally able to come to grips with the

★For a fuller account of these Bible translation principles, see *Translating the Word of God,* by John Beekman and John Callow, Zondervan, 1974.

new translation principles was the very location of the workshop site. It rested on a slight rise overlooking irrigated fields of brilliant green alfalfa and corn. Less than a mile away, the ancient village of Ixmiquilpan, dominated by an imposing church built shortly after the conquest of Mexico, was flanked by colorful outdoor markets and cobblestone streets and ringed with high irregular mountains that changed into different hues of purple with the rising and setting of the desert sun. All this captured his imagination, and he wanted to share his experience with his friends in Barrow and Wainwright. But when he took up his pen to write, he frequently found himself groping for new words and new ways to express all that was new around him. His friends, many of whom were his age and older, had little understanding of cactus and maguey plants, irrigation, and ordered fields of corn that would one day be ground into *masa* for tortillas. There were "domesticated" dogs in his friends' experience, but few could relate to chickens, pigs, sheep, oxen, and burros. And as Roy searched for meaningful ways to express in Inupiatun the new world of the Otomi desert, he came to understand how practical and important it was to indeed translate the Scriptures with more attention to meaning than form.

Slowly at first and then with vigor, Roy accepted Don's proposal that in order to make the best use of his time and talents they should divide and conquer. Working with no less than five difficult commentaries and three different translations of the Bible plus his own understanding of what the Inupiat language could convey, Don thoroughly researched each passage of Scripture for its essential meaning, then put these concepts into an Eskimoized English text.

Don then presented the block of material to Roy for his review and evaluation. After a thorough discussion of the passage, and after reaching unanimity about what the passage meant, Roy proceeded to translate Don's Eskimoized text into readable and intelligible Inupiatun. Thus the two men worked simultaneously. Don did the research and exposition of the text and worked hard to stay one step ahead of Roy who translated the Eskimoized English version into "good" Inupiatun.

So enthusiastic were the two men over this new method, they began a fresh clean translation of the Inupiat New Testament. In effect, they jettisoned their old translation. When they explained to John what they were doing and how they were going about it, he nodded his head in approval and smiled his boyish mischievous smile. This was exactly what he had hoped and planned would happen all along, but believing self-correction is the best correction, he had let Don and Roy make their own discovery.

When the workshop ended and Roy was about to leave, he clasped John's hand and said, "This experience has meant more to me than anything else I ever learned about the Bible, including my seminary training. I have learned more in these days than I ever thought possible for an old man to learn. Before Don and I weren't sure where we were going. We were often frustrated. But now we indeed know what to do and how to get there."

After two years of almost nonstop work at Wycliffe's Fairbanks center, Roy, Don, and Thelma completed the Inupiat New Testament and sent it off to the publishers. It was April 1967.

Two years earlier when Don had written to Roy and asked him for his help and commitment of a full year to the translation project, Roy's response had been like Jesus' instructions to His followers when asked for a favor. Only in this case, instead of going an extra mile, Roy went an extra year. But there was more. In his letter to Roy, Don had expressed his sorrow over the translation not being accepted for publication and how deeply he felt for Roy's hurt and disappointment. To that letter, Roy had responded with this letter of reassurance:

> Don, don't feel so bad and too sympathetic about me. I feel the Lord is with us riding in the boat and will help us to ride to the other side of the translation work. As I told an elder, I am either a hardened old sinner, which I hope and pray I am not, or I am mature enough to take things that oppose or hinder in the way the Lord took them when He walked on earth.
>
> Perhaps some of us have become too proud or boastful and the Lord has caused or rather allowed someone to throw a monkey wrench into the cogs of the wheel, thus causing us to be put back into the rightful place of humbleness and a deeper prayer life. So I've gotten my loins girded and sleeves rolled and ready to go back to the work the Lord had planned for me from the beginning. And as the song says, "I intend to go through."

By God's grace and help, Roy Ahmaogak did go through and rejoiced that the dream of a lifetime was at last a reality. For the first time in their long and often painful history, the Inupiat would have the Book of Books to give them truth and insight into the meaning of life and death. God's Word in the Inupiatun language would put an end forever to mere opinions about God and His will for man, and this Truth, this Gospel, would be housed in the most meaningful of all containers—the beautiful and comfortable Inupiatun language. And Roy was happy.

All that was lacking now was for the New Testament to be printed and dedicated and for Roy to hold the bound volume in his own hands. In the meantime, he returned to Wainwright to wait and enjoy again the leisurely hunt. He had come full circle. It seemed God was giving him the satisfaction of doing in sweetness what he had as a young man given up, at first in rebellion, so many years before. Truly the promise of his life verse, Galatians 1:15–16b, had come to pass: "God, who set me apart from birth and called me by his grace, was pleased to reveal his Son in me so that I might preach him among the Gentiles . . ."

In the midst of his various honors (first and youngest Eskimo elder to be ordained in the Presbyterian church, then pastor, and then being conferred with an honorary doctorate from Whitworth College, plus the privilege of extensive travel), Roy never allowed himself to forget his humble beginnings, nor God's grace in his life. In part of an extraordinary and deeply insightful message he gave to his fellow Bible translators at the Ixmiquilpan workshop, Roy revealed just how deeply he felt about his roots and God's grace:

By God's grace, I came into being at Barrow, in 1898. According to my mother's history the good news of the Gospel was still much of a mystery among our people (and my parents). The story of the Gospel was only about eight years in existence around Barrow and Wainwright and our people still believed and practiced many taboos and superstitious beliefs. All my children were born in the hospital,★ but not me. When I was born, our people thought a woman was unclean when she gave birth. So when the time came for my mother to deliver me, she was taken out of her warm sod hut and put inside a small snow igloo. The only heat inside the snow house was from a small stone lamp that burned seal oil. The wick for the seal oil lamp was just a piece of moss. Not very much heat when the temperature often went down to minus fifty-one degrees.

★Roy's family consisted of twelve natural children plus one adopted child. He said he lost count of his grandchildren after fifty-three, but he did remember that he had nine great grandchildren.

From my mother's history, she told me that for four days after I was born, her food and water were pushed in through an opening so she could reach it. And the only way her husband and friends could find out if she was well was to call from the outside when they brought her food. Our people believed that if anyone came in contact with a woman when she was giving birth, they would become unclean and subject to some mysterious tragedy or severe sickness accompanied with death. No one was allowed ever to help or assist with the birth of a child.

This is why I say it was only by God's grace that I survived those first three or four days in the snow igloo until my mother was considered clean and taken back into the sod hut. My mother told me I had nine brothers and sisters, all older than myself, but all died at an early age.

Later when my mother married a second time, her new husband had his own four children and all of these died at the time when the village was overrun with tuberculosis. I lost my first wife with TB and my mother's two brothers also died from TB.

As I look back and ponder upon those years when I was living closely with those who had TB, I marvel that my health was not affected. Is it any wonder that I say to you today that it is only by God's grace that I stand before you with no sign of illness?

This is why Galatians 1:15-16 has become so important to me. Truly I feel it was God who separated me from my mother's womb and called me by His grace to be His servant to tell my people about the good news of Jesus Christ. Truly our Lord has visited me with great kindness all the days of my life.

And part of that kindness was being allowed to return in retirement to Wainwright, satisfied that the work God had commissioned him to do was at last completed. Now in the tranquility and peace that comes after struggle, Roy, without anxiety, could doze over a steaming mug of tea or chomp on a piece of *muktuk* while a pot of caribou steaks simmered on the stove and the wind blasted the harsh land and whistled around the eaves of his house. Or if he wanted, he could sit all day in a duck blind to wait the heavy beating of air that signaled a flock of eider ducks overhead.

Consequently, when Roy learned of his son Freddy's intention to go caribou hunting on that day in January 1968, Roy insisted on going along.

"You have been sick and indoors for ten days with a bad, bad cold," reminded Isobel, his wife. "You should not go."

But the pressure, or the instinct, was too great. And in spite of Isobel hiding his parka (which he found), Roy and Freddy took off across the tundra, each in their snow machines in search of caribou.

Isobel was right, of course. Roy shouldn't have gone, because about eight hours later, an exhausted Freddy struggled to get his collapsed father into the house.

"We must get Papa to hospital in Barrow," said Freddy. "He started to get worse as we went farther and farther out onto the tundra. Only when he collapsed and went into this delirium could I bring him back. It has almost been impossible for me to drive the snow machine and hold Papa at the same time. He is as heavy as a polar bear."

For several days after his arrival at the Barrow hospital, Roy hovered between life and death. And then on about the fifth day, the doctor reported an increased sign of strength. "He has a severe case of pneumonia," said the doctor to Don. (Don was staying for a short time at the Presbyterian manse, just a 100 yards from the hospital, working on literacy materials.) "He is still weak, yet even with only a half of one lung with which to breathe, I think the worst is over."

It was welcome news indeed, and Don along with Isobel and Roy's family and many friends heaved thankful sighs of relief. Relaxed in the belief he was going to get well, Don and the others were totally unprepared for the next event.

About 7:00 P.M., on February 1, 1968, just one week after Roy was admitted to the hospital, a young Eskimo boy, without knocking, burst through Don's door at the manse and blurted out, "Ahmaogak *tukuruk!*" (Ahmaogak is dead!)

Roy dead? "It can't be true," said Don in disbelief. "How can it be true?"

But it was true. A nurse, in preparing Roy for visitors, had left a glass of mouthwash for him, then left to attend another patient. Mistaking the mouthwash for something to drink, Roy drank it and, as we often say, it went down the wrong way. He began to choke and because he had only a half lung with which to breathe, the extra pressure collapsed this lung and deprived Roy of life-giving air.

Immediately after receiving the news, Don raced to Roy's bedside and found Isobel and a surprisingly large number of friends and relatives who had already gathered. Most of them were weeping and wailing and Don had to shout over the confusion. "I would like to pray," he said. In a moment, the loud weeping and wailing turned to quiet sobs. And through his own tears, Don prayed for God to comfort and strengthen the family and friends of this strong and kindly servant of God.

At the funeral on February 2, Don read 2 Timothy 4:7-8:

I have fought the good fight, I have finished the race, I have kept the faith. Now there is in store for me the crown of righteousness, which the Lord, the righteous Judge, will reward to me on that day, and not only to me, but also to all who have longed for his appearing.

This was a difficult reading for Don, particularly when he thought about the Inupiat New Testament dedication just eight months away. It seemed so terribly strange to face that important and historic event without the man who, in many ways, had become a father figure to him and the man most responsible for its completion.

When news of Roy's death reached the outside world, dozens of sympathy letters and anecdotes poured into the little house in Wainwright and to Don personally. One of them came from Dr. Eugene Nida who had taught Roy to swim during the summer he took his linguistic training at the Summer Institute of Linguistics in 1946:

> We are terribly sorry to hear of Roy's death. He always seemed so young and vigorous. I know it must be a great disappointment to his family not to have him present for the completion of the publication of the New Testament to which he gave so many years of his life . . . I am sure the New Testament, which he was able to complete with your help, will be one of the greatest heritages of his people.

And from a man who was a correspondent for the Barrow *Tundra Times* and who almost fifty years earlier had been hired by Roy to accompany him and Isobel on that historic dog sled trip to Demarcation Point to take a census came the following:

> It was a great shock when I learned that my old friend Dr. Roy Ahmaogak passed away. I will never forget that trip to Demarcation Point in the 1920s. On our way we ran out of flour and sugar and food for the dogs.
>
> One morning I was leading our dogs and Roy and his wife were in the sled and I happened to see a ptarmigan ahead of me. I stopped and waited until Roy got out of the sled and came to where I was standing. The ptarmigan was

about a hundred feet away and Roy shot it. Immediately I started after it. But before I could reach it, an owl grabbed the dead ptarmigan and flew away with it. Oh, what a pity when all of us could have used that good broth to warm our bones!

But all was not lost. Two days later we came to a camp and the people treated us well. They fed us and our dogs and we were happy again.

Roy traveled a lot when he was young and was a mighty hunter both in game and men. Now Roy is no longer with us, but someday we who remain will also pass away like our beloved friend. Friends, we will never know when this will happen. But when it does, those of us who know Jesus will see each other face to face.

Still another who had sung in Roy's choir and who was a teen-ager in the young people's class he taught, said:

Roy Ahmaogak was strong. You could tell by his presence. You knew what he said was right. You didn't even need to hear him speak; you could tell by the way he carried himself and by his attitude that he had a deep faith in God. And when he did speak, you could tell that his faith was important and that he lived by the words he spoke.

Roy's son Freddy had always known that his father's faith was important, but never just how important until he was out on the tundra when his father was passing in and out of his delirium. Said Freddy:

It was late when I got him back to the house. And we had to wait until the next morning for the plane to come and pick him up. But all the time we were out on the tundra and during the long night, he kept mumbling over and over from Hebrews, chapter 13, verses 5 and 6: "I will never leave you or forsake you . . . I will never leave you or forsake you. Therefore, I will not fear what man will do to me." My father was a man of great physical strength, but his true strength was his spiritual strength. His actions matched his words. It was the Word of God in his heart and mind that made him truly a man of strength.

On a cold raw day, October 13, 1968, in the Barrow Presbyterian Church, the Inupiat New Testament was finally dedicated. While Don wished Roy could have been part of the joy and honor of that moment, he could not help but be encouraged by Abel's epitaph as recorded in Hebrews 11:4b: "And by faith he still speaks, even though he is dead."

Afterword:
You Know You Promised

The letter came as a complete surprise and overwhelming shock to Thelma. It was from the then president of Wycliffe Bible Translators, Dr. George Cowan.

"I don't understand how he can be serious!" said Thelma. "Africa? Ivory Coast? It's so hot there, especially for us after living the past twelve years in the Arctic."

"George Cowan never makes idle proposals," said Don. "Ivory Coast is a new field for SIL and they need experienced personnel for administration and to oversee the Bible translation program. George would like us to prayerfully consider going there. He wants to make me the new branch director."

Thelma shook her head incredulously. "I can hardly believe this." And then in the middle of her head-shaking, she gave Don one of her whimsical cat-swallowed-the-mouse smiles. "You know, it just dawned on me that God may be asking me to keep my promise."

"Promise? What promise?" asked Don.

"The promise I made to God when I first began my nurse's training," said Thelma. "I promised I would go anywhere, even to Africa, if He would help me through my studies."

"And did God help you get through your training?" asked Don with a broad smile.

"I'm afraid He did," said Thelma.

"Then it's settled?" asked Don.

"I know I promised to go anywhere, even to Africa," said Thelma, "but I believe we need to pray about this before we give George our final answer."

That prayer meeting lasted four months, and in April 1970, Don and Thelma sent out a letter announcing their decision and future plans:

> What does Alaska have in common with Africa? Not much. But because Wycliffe needs experienced personnel to help in setting up and getting new branches started, we have accepted the challenge, the challenge to participate in Wycliffe's Ivory Coast Branch.
>
> Some have asked us why we are leaving Alaska after we have spent so many years learning the Inupiat language. Normally when a translator finishes a New Testament, he spends time in literacy work or moves to a neighboring dialect. We have no close Eskimo dialect to move to and we've spent considerable time working with the Bureau of Indian Affairs writing a cultural enrichment course to be used in the eighth grade Social Studies course. Further, we have been involved in other literacy programs to promote reading, particularly of the New Testament.

The Websters went on to explain how through the efforts of themselves and Roy Ahmaogak, there was a self-teaching reading course available in all the villages. And in each village there was at least one person who was holding reading classes.

The letter ended with their travel plans—a summer

in Canada, then on to Paris, France, to brush up on their French (Ivory Coast is French speaking) and to Ivory Coast in early 1971. Finally, there was one last verse of Scripture as a kind of personal idiograph of the Websters:

"No man having put his hand to the plow and looking back is fit for the kingdom of God." Dear friends, we pray that you will help us advance in His name, not fearing the unknown, realizing that God never gives us a job beyond His enabling power. And pray for our Eskimo friends.

Through two long, often difficult four-year terms in Ivory Coast,★ the Websters never forgot the Inupiat people. How could they? So many had become friends, good friends.

Until the writing of this book, Don never believed he would ever again have the opportunity to visit his Inupiat friends. But in September 1980, before freeze-up, and with this author in tow, Don, after an absence of twelve years, found himself once again walking down the gravel streets of Barrow, Alaska. The following are his feelings and observations of that visit.

"I was amazed to see what twelve years and the discovery of oil had done to the Arctic and its people. In the place of ice cellars, most people stored their caribou meat in large indoor freezers. Most homes had a color television set with twelve channels beamed in by satellite. For those not interested in watching the tube, Barrow sported a 12,000-watt radio station.

"I was struck by the absence of skin boats and dog teams. These have been replaced by motor launches,

★Don and Thelma, plus Julie and Becky, experienced in different ways the same high drama and testings as they had experienced in the Arctic. Their outstanding service to that branch is worthy of another book.

snow machines, and balloon-tired motorbikes. In fact, there were so many motorbikes and other cars and trucks that I needed to be careful crossing the street.

"There was a four-story office building of modern design that housed the regional government facilities and a two-level open office complex artistically arranged around a minimuseum of Inupiat artifacts.

"For a social evening out, overlooking the ice-clogged Arctic Ocean was Pepi's Restaurant. For the often bleak Arctic, this provided a warm international diversion, as well as serving outstanding Latin American meals. And just a stone's throw from the restaurant was a modern two-story shopping center that sold everything from nails to nailpolish and food to hunting equipment. Everything seemed such a contrast from the early sixties when we lived in Wainwright and used Barrow as a jumping off place. Now in a matter of seconds, I was able to pick up the telephone and talk to some old friends in Wainwright Village. As I did, I thought of the many frustrating times Thelma and I had stood beside the schoolteacher while he fiddled with the shortwave radio in an attempt to get some crucial information from the doctor in Barrow.

"While many of the external elements of the community had changed, the deep pragmatic Inupiat spirit had not. I observed the same brave and aggressive skill needed to tackle the gigantic bowhead whale transferred to meeting the penetration of the twentieth century western culture. In an educational center, bright young educators were adapting the Eskimo language to handle new objects and concepts. And when I saw the handsome new books and reading materials, my mind flashed back to our one-room home in Wainwright Village. There Thelma and I had, with our hand-operated mimeograph, 'printed' the first editions of our own reading materials. These we tested in trial literacy classes just one month after Mary Ellen went to heaven. Now in order for the materials to be more fully developed, I was asked and happily consented to sign over all my copyrights to this education council.

"Thus while I noticed that material accumulations marked a change, I also noted that the change often was only superficial. Underneath was the same accepting, uncomplicated Inupiat character. This came out one afternoon when Hugh Steven and myself joined a group of Inupiat friends on the ice floes to fish for tomcod.

"After the initial greetings, everyone became totally absorbed in the scintillating challenge of hooking these feisty six-inch fish. With good-natured teasing, of the kind I remembered from so many years before, the people laughed and chuckled whenever someone flopped a fish out onto the ice. But when someone lost a hooked fish, then the teasing and laughter was at its richest.

"Not one of these Inupiat needed to catch the tomcod. They had the means to buy a variety of frozen fish at the supermarket. But they were Inupiat, and in the face of natural gas-heated homes, modern technology, and space-age gadgetry, they needed to pursue this age-old custom and sport. Their Inupiatness demanded it.

"While this was true, I also saw that alcohol and drugs had taken their toll among a number of the younger people. This grieved me, as did the report that some of the young people were attempting to revive the pre-Christian animism of their ancestors. All this reminded me that we face a strong enemy who goes around like a roaring lion seeking whom he may devour.

"But in the face of all this, I found people everywhere who were open to the ministry of God's Word. And I saw with gladness the translated Scriptures being used in public worship and in private homes.

"One afternoon I visited Helen, an older Inupiat

woman. After telling me the sad and tragic news of a relative who had been murdered and how this had shocked her, she concluded with, 'But I read the New Testament and I think about God and stay happy.' (I noticed her Inupiat New Testament was well worn and she had several colored wool threads affixed to the binding for bookmarks.)

"It was deeply gratifying to return to the Arctic. I saw Roy's life goal of the New Testament in his own language being used effectively, and when I thought of my and Thelma's part in that project and realized the Word was living and producing results, I thanked God for allowing us the privilege of being a part of the Inupiat translation program.

"As I left Barrow and the plane took me back to my own world as Associate Pastor of Forward Baptist Church in Cambridge, Ontario, my mind flew back to the dedication of the Inupiat New Testament. One of the first people to buy the book was old Negovana, a man who had known the hard times when people starved to death because they missed the yearly migrations. With a smile as big as an Arctic sunburst, he held out his New Testament and said, 'Now God's Word is in Eskimo, me no starve no more.' "